How to Write a Business Plan

Table of Contents

CW01501610

Introduction

The importance of a business plan

The importance of a business plan cannot be overstated when it comes to starting or growing a successful business. A well-thought-out and comprehensive business plan serves as a roadmap that guides entrepreneurs through the various stages of business development, helping them make informed decisions and stay focused on their goals. Let's delve deeper into the significance of having a business plan:

1. Strategic Direction: One of the primary benefits of a business plan is that it provides a clear strategic direction for the business. By outlining the company's mission, vision, goals, and strategies, the plan helps align all stakeholders towards a common purpose. It serves as a blueprint for decision-making and helps entrepreneurs stay on track amidst challenges and opportunities.

2. Funding and Investment: For startups and businesses looking to secure funding or investment, a well-developed business plan is essential. Investors and lenders often require a detailed business plan to evaluate the viability and potential of the business. A strong business plan can help attract investors by showcasing the market opportunity, competitive advantage, financial projections, and growth strategies.

3. Operational Efficiency: A business plan outlines the key operational and organizational aspects of the business, including business structure, staffing, facilities, technology, and processes. By clearly defining these operational components, entrepreneurs can streamline their operations, optimize resources, and improve efficiency.

4. Risk Management: Through tools like SWOT analysis and market research, a business plan helps identify potential risks and challenges that the business may face. By anticipating these risks, entrepreneurs can develop contingency plans and mitigation strategies to minimize their impact on the business.

5. Goal Setting and Monitoring: Setting specific, measurable, achievable, relevant, and time-bound (SMART) goals is crucial for business success. A business plan helps entrepreneurs set realistic targets for growth, revenue, market share, and other key performance indicators. Regularly monitoring progress against these goals allows for adjustments and course corrections as needed.

6. Communication and Alignment: A well-crafted business plan serves as a communication tool for internal and external stakeholders. Internally, it helps align employees, managers, and partners towards common objectives. Externally, it conveys the business's vision, value proposition, and growth potential to customers, suppliers, and other external parties.

7. Long-Term Planning: Business planning is not just about short-term goals but also about long-term sustainability and growth. A business plan forces entrepreneurs to think strategically about the future of their business, consider industry trends, and adapt to changing market conditions.

In conclusion, a business plan is not just a document; it is a dynamic tool that guides entrepreneurs through the intricacies of business management, from conceptualization to implementation. By investing time and effort into developing a comprehensive business plan, entrepreneurs can increase their chances of success, mitigate risks, attract investors, and ultimately achieve their business goals.

Overview of what a business plan should achieve

The overview of what a business plan should achieve is a crucial aspect of understanding the purpose and importance of creating a comprehensive and effective business plan. A well-crafted business plan serves as a roadmap for the success and sustainability of a business venture, guiding entrepreneurs through the process of starting, growing, and managing their business. In this section, we will delve into the key objectives and goals that a business plan should aim to achieve.

1. Strategic Direction and Clarity: One of the fundamental purposes of a business plan is to provide a clear and concise overview of the business concept, mission, vision, and objectives. By defining these elements, entrepreneurs can establish a strategic direction for their business and align all activities and decisions towards achieving their long-term goals.

2. Communication Tool: A business plan serves as a powerful communication tool for internal and external stakeholders, including employees, investors, lenders, and partners. It conveys the business idea, value proposition, market positioning, and growth strategies in a structured and organized manner, facilitating effective communication and alignment of goals among all parties involved.

3. Planning and Forecasting: A well-developed business plan enables entrepreneurs to conduct thorough research, analysis, and forecasting to assess the feasibility and viability of their business idea. By outlining financial projections, market opportunities, competitive landscape, and operational strategies, entrepreneurs can make informed decisions and plan for the future growth and success of their business.

4. Risk Management and Contingency Planning: Business plans also play a crucial role in identifying potential risks, challenges, and uncertainties that may impact the business operations. By conducting a SWOT analysis, competitive analysis, and market research, entrepreneurs can proactively identify risks and develop contingency plans to mitigate potential threats and capitalize on opportunities in the market.

5. Resource Allocation and Budgeting: Another key objective of a business plan is to outline the resource requirements, funding needs, and budget allocation for different aspects of the business, such as marketing, operations, technology, and staffing. By clearly defining the financial aspects of the business, entrepreneurs can effectively manage resources, track expenses, and optimize profitability.

6. Monitoring and Performance Measurement: A business plan should also include key performance indicators (KPIs) and milestones that enable entrepreneurs to track progress, evaluate performance, and measure the success of their business against predefined goals and objectives. Regular monitoring and performance measurement help in identifying areas of improvement, adapting strategies, and making informed decisions to drive business growth.

In conclusion, a well-crafted business plan should aim to achieve strategic direction, effective communication, thorough planning and forecasting, risk management, resource allocation, and performance measurement. By setting clear objectives and goals, entrepreneurs can create a roadmap for success, attract investors and partners, and navigate the challenges of starting and growing a business with confidence and clarity.

What you will gain from this guide

In the book "How to Write a Business Plan," readers can expect to gain a comprehensive understanding and practical guidance on creating an effective business plan that serves as a roadmap for success. This guide provides valuable insights and tools for entrepreneurs, business owners, and aspiring professionals looking to launch or grow a business. Here are some key takeaways that readers can expect to gain from this guide:

1. Clarity on the Importance of a Business Plan: Understanding the significance of having a well-thought-out business plan is crucial for any business endeavor. This guide will emphasize the role of a business plan in setting clear objectives, defining strategies, and ensuring the overall success of a business.

2. Step-by-Step Approach: The guide offers a structured and step-by-step approach to creating a business plan, starting from understanding the purpose of a business plan to conducting research and analysis, crafting an executive summary, describing the company, outlining products or services, developing a market strategy, detailing operations, creating a financial plan, and preparing for review and presentation.

3. Knowledge on Different Types of Business Plans: Readers will learn about different types of business plans such as traditional, lean, and internal plans, and understand how to choose the right format based on their specific needs and audience.

4. Insight into Research and Analysis Techniques: The guide delves into various research and analysis techniques including market research, industry analysis, customer analysis, SWOT analysis, and competitive analysis. Readers will learn how to gather valuable information to make informed decisions and develop effective strategies.

5. Practical Tips for Tailoring the Business Plan: Understanding how to tailor a business plan to different audiences, whether it be investors, lenders, or internal stakeholders, is essential for effectively communicating the vision and potential of the business.

6. Guidance on Crafting Essential Sections: Readers will gain insights into crafting essential sections of a business plan such as the executive summary, company description, products or services, market strategy, operations plan, financial plan, and appendices, ensuring a comprehensive and well-rounded document.

7. Financial Planning Skills: The guide provides readers with the knowledge and tools to create financial statements, revenue models, funding requirements, financial projections, and break-even analysis, helping them to develop a solid financial plan for their business.

8. Tips for Review, Presentation, and Ongoing Planning: Readers will learn techniques for reviewing and revising their business plan, seeking feedback, finalizing the document, presenting it to stakeholders, and updating the plan as the business evolves, ensuring that the plan remains relevant and aligned with the business goals.

Overall, this guide equips readers with the necessary knowledge, skills, and tools to develop a comprehensive and effective business plan that serves as a strategic blueprint for success. By following the step-by-step approach outlined in this guide, readers will be empowered to articulate their business vision, attract potential investors, and navigate the complexities of running a successful business with clarity and confidence.

Chapter 1

Understanding the Purpose of a Business Plan

Defining a Business Plan

A business plan is a comprehensive document that outlines the goals, strategies, and operational details of a business. It serves as a roadmap for entrepreneurs, guiding them through the process of starting, managing, and growing their business. A well-crafted business plan is essential for any business, whether it is a startup seeking funding or an established company looking to expand.

At its core, a business plan is a formal statement of business goals, the reasons they are attainable, and the plan for reaching those goals. It provides a clear overview of the business concept, including the products or services offered, the target market, competition analysis, marketing strategies, operational processes, and financial projections.

One of the primary reasons why a business plan matters is that it serves as a communication tool. It allows entrepreneurs to convey their vision and strategy to potential investors, partners, employees, and other stakeholders. A well-written business plan can help attract investors by demonstrating the viability and growth potential of the business. It also provides a framework for decision-making and accountability within the organization.

A business plan is not just a document for external stakeholders; it also serves as a guide for the business owner. By clearly defining the business goals and strategies, a business plan helps entrepreneurs stay focused and make informed decisions. It provides a roadmap for achieving short-term objectives and long-term vision, helping to align resources and efforts towards a common goal.

Furthermore, a business plan acts as a tool for risk management. By conducting thorough market research, analyzing competitors, and identifying potential challenges, entrepreneurs can anticipate risks and develop contingency plans to mitigate them. This proactive approach can help businesses navigate uncertainties and adapt to changing market conditions.

In addition, a business plan is crucial for financial planning and management. It includes detailed financial projections, such as revenue forecasts, expense estimates, and cash flow analysis. These financial projections help entrepreneurs determine the funding requirements, assess the profitability of the business, and track performance against targets. By regularly reviewing and updating the financial projections, businesses can make informed decisions to optimize their financial resources.

Overall, a business plan is a valuable tool for guiding the strategic direction of a business, securing funding, managing operations, and achieving long-term success. It encapsulates the vision, mission, and values of the business, providing a framework for growth and sustainability. Whether you are a new entrepreneur or an experienced business owner, investing time and effort in developing a comprehensive business plan is essential for building a successful and thriving enterprise.

Types of Business Plans

In the realm of business planning, it is essential to understand the different types of business plans available and how they can serve various purposes depending on the needs of the business. Three common types of business plans are traditional business plans, lean startup plans, and internal business plans. Each type has its own unique characteristics and is tailored to specific situations and audiences.

1. Traditional Business Plans:

Traditional business plans are comprehensive and detailed documents that outline all aspects of a business. They typically include detailed sections on market research, competition analysis, financial projections, and operational strategies. Traditional business plans are commonly used when seeking external funding from investors, banks, or other financial institutions.

Key features of traditional business plans include:

- In-depth market analysis to understand the industry landscape and potential opportunities.
- Detailed financial projections covering revenue forecasts, expenses, and cash flow.
- Comprehensive operational plans outlining how the business will be structured and managed.
- Focus on long-term goals and strategies for sustainable growth and profitability.

Traditional business plans are ideal for businesses looking to secure substantial funding or seeking to provide a comprehensive roadmap for growth and development. They are typically more formal and structured compared to other types of business plans.

2. Lean Startup Plans:

Lean startup plans are streamlined and focused on testing business ideas quickly and efficiently. These plans are popular among startups and early-stage businesses that prioritize agility and flexibility in their planning process. Lean startup plans emphasize experimentation, rapid iteration, and learning from customer feedback.

Key features of lean startup plans include:

- Minimalistic approach with a focus on core business elements.

- Rapid testing of assumptions through prototyping and customer validation.
- Flexible strategies that can be easily adjusted based on market feedback.
- Emphasis on identifying and addressing key risks and uncertainties.

Lean startup plans are designed to help entrepreneurs validate their business concepts before investing significant time and resources. By focusing on the essential elements of the business model, lean startup plans enable quick decision-making and adaptation to changing market conditions.

3. Internal Business Plans:

Internal business plans are strategic documents used by businesses to align internal teams and departments towards common goals and objectives. Unlike traditional business plans, internal plans are not intended for external audiences like investors or lenders. Instead, they serve as a roadmap for internal stakeholders to guide decision-making and resource allocation.

Key features of internal business plans include:
- Clear communication of business goals and priorities to employees.
- Detailed action plans and timelines for executing strategic initiatives.
- Alignment of departmental objectives with overall business objectives.
- Emphasis on fostering collaboration and cross-functional teamwork.

Internal business plans are valuable tools for fostering a shared vision and driving organizational alignment. By outlining clear objectives and strategies, internal plans help employees understand their roles in achieving business success and contribute to a cohesive and coordinated approach to business operations.

In conclusion, understanding the differences between traditional, lean startup, and internal business plans is crucial for selecting the most appropriate planning approach for your business. Whether you are seeking external funding, testing a new business idea, or aligning internal teams, choosing the right type of business plan can significantly impact the success and sustainability of your business venture. By tailoring your business plan to your specific needs and audience, you can create a roadmap that guides your business towards achieving its goals and objectives effectively.

Uses of a Business Plan

The business plan is a crucial document that serves multiple purposes for entrepreneurs and business owners alike. Understanding the various uses of a business plan is essential for maximizing its effectiveness in different aspects of business management and growth. In this section, we will delve into the three primary uses of a business plan: securing funding, guiding business operations, and strategic planning.

1. Securing Funding:

One of the most common and critical uses of a business plan is to secure funding from investors, banks, or other financial institutions. A well-crafted business plan acts as a roadmap that demonstrates the viability and potential profitability of the business to potential investors. It provides insight into the business concept, market opportunity, competitive landscape, financial projections, and growth strategies. Investors and lenders rely on the business plan to assess the risk and return potential of investing in the business. A comprehensive financial plan within the business plan outlines the funding requirements, expected revenue streams, expenses, and projected profitability, giving investors confidence in the business's financial viability.

2. Guiding Business Operations:

Beyond its role in securing funding, a business plan serves as a strategic tool for guiding day-to-day operations and decision-making within the organization. By outlining the business's mission, vision, objectives, and strategies, the plan aligns all stakeholders towards common goals and objectives. The components of the business plan, such as the company description, products or services, market strategy, and operations plan, provide a comprehensive overview of the business's structure, offerings, target market, marketing and sales strategies, operational processes, and resource requirements. This information helps business owners and managers make informed decisions, allocate resources effectively, and stay focused on achieving key milestones and objectives.

3. Strategic Planning:
In addition to guiding immediate operations, the business plan plays a crucial role in long-term strategic planning. By conducting a thorough analysis of the market, industry trends, competition, and internal capabilities through tools like SWOT analysis and market research, businesses can identify growth opportunities, potential threats, and competitive advantages. This strategic insight helps businesses develop actionable strategies for sustainable growth, market expansion, product innovation, and competitive positioning. The financial projections and break-even analysis within the business plan enable businesses to set realistic goals, track progress, and adjust strategies as needed to stay on course towards long-term success.

In conclusion, the business plan is a versatile tool that serves multiple purposes in the business management and growth process. From securing funding to guiding day-to-day operations and informing strategic planning, a well-developed business plan is essential for setting a clear direction, attracting investors, and achieving sustainable growth. Business owners and entrepreneurs should view the business plan as a dynamic document that evolves with the business, requiring regular review, updates, and adjustments to reflect changing market conditions, business objectives, and growth opportunities.

Components of a Business Plan

A well-structured business plan is essential for guiding the growth and success of a business. Understanding the key components of a business plan and their respective roles is crucial for creating a comprehensive and effective strategic document. In this section, we will delve into the main sections that make up a typical business plan and discuss their significance in shaping the overall strategy of a business.

1. Executive Summary:

The executive summary serves as a snapshot of the entire business plan, providing a concise overview of the business concept, goals, market opportunity, financial highlights, and key insights. It acts as the first impression for readers, highlighting the most critical aspects of the plan and enticing them to delve deeper into the details. The executive summary is crucial for capturing the attention of potential investors, lenders, or stakeholders and should be compelling and impactful.

2. Company Description:

The company description section outlines essential details about the business itself, including its structure, mission, vision, business model, location, and legal considerations. This section provides context for the rest of the business plan, giving readers a clear understanding of the business's purpose, goals, and operating environment. By defining the core elements of the business, the company description sets the foundation for the strategic direction and operations of the company.

3. Products or Services:

In this section, businesses outline the specifics of the products or services they offer, including detailed descriptions, unique selling propositions, development stages, pricing strategies, and intellectual property considerations. By articulating the value proposition of their offerings and differentiating them from competitors, businesses can demonstrate their market relevance and competitive advantage. This section is critical for showcasing the core offerings of the business and explaining how they meet the needs of target customers.

4. Market Strategy:

The market strategy section details the marketing and sales strategies that the business will employ to attract and retain customers. It includes elements such as the marketing plan, branding strategy, sales process, customer acquisition tactics, and advertising and promotion strategies. By outlining how the business plans to reach and engage its target market, this section provides a roadmap for driving growth and building a strong customer base. A well-defined market strategy is essential for effectively positioning the business in the marketplace and driving revenue generation.

5. Operations Plan:

The operations plan outlines the day-to-day processes, supply chain management, technology and equipment requirements, staffing and human resources strategies, and quality control measures of the business. This section provides insight into how the business will operate efficiently and deliver its products or services to customers. By detailing the operational workflows and resource requirements, businesses can ensure that their operations are well-structured and aligned with their strategic objectives.

6. Financial Plan:

The financial plan section presents the financial statements, revenue model, funding requirements, financial projections, and break-even analysis of the business. It provides a comprehensive overview of the financial health and viability of the business, showcasing its revenue potential, capital needs, and profitability forecasts. The financial plan is crucial for demonstrating the financial feasibility of the business and attracting potential investors or lenders. It also serves as a roadmap for managing the financial aspects of the business and monitoring its performance over time.

In conclusion, each component of a business plan plays a vital role in shaping the overall strategy and direction of a business. By carefully crafting each section and ensuring they are well-integrated and aligned with the overarching goals of the business, entrepreneurs can create a robust and compelling business plan that serves as a roadmap for success. A well-structured business plan not only guides decision-making and operations but also communicates the vision and potential of the business to external stakeholders, paving the way for growth and sustainability.

How to Tailor a Business Plan

Adapting a business plan to suit the specific needs and expectations of different audiences is a crucial aspect of creating a successful and effective document. Tailoring your business plan to investors, lenders, and internal stakeholders involves understanding their perspectives, priorities, and requirements. By customizing the content and presentation of your plan, you can increase the chances of securing funding, gaining support, and aligning your team towards common goals.

1. Investors:

Investors are primarily concerned with the potential return on their investment and the level of risk associated with your business. When tailoring your business plan for investors, focus on highlighting the revenue-generating potential of your venture, showcasing a clear path to profitability, and demonstrating a solid understanding of market opportunities and competitive dynamics. Emphasize key financial metrics such as revenue projections, profit margins, and return on investment (ROI). Investors also want to see a well-defined exit strategy, outlining how they can realize their investment in the future. Use language that is concise, compelling, and backed up by data to instill confidence in potential investors.

2. Lenders:

Lenders, such as banks or financial institutions, are more interested in the ability of your business to generate cash flow and repay loans on time. When tailoring your business plan for lenders, focus on providing detailed financial projections, including cash flow forecasts, balance sheets, and debt repayment schedules. Highlight the stability of your business model, the strength of your revenue streams, and the measures in place to mitigate financial risks. Lenders also look for collateral to secure their loans, so be prepared to discuss any assets that can be used as security for the loan. Clearly articulate the purpose of the loan, the terms of repayment, and the potential impact on your cash flow.

3. Internal Stakeholders:

Internal stakeholders, including employees, managers, and board members, are interested in how the business plan aligns with the overall strategic goals and operational priorities of the organization. When tailoring your business plan for internal stakeholders, focus on fostering buy-in, alignment, and accountability within the organization. Clearly communicate how each department or team contributes to the overall business objectives and how success will be measured. Customize the plan to address specific concerns or priorities of different internal stakeholders, such as operational efficiency, employee engagement, or innovation. Encourage feedback and collaboration to ensure that the business plan reflects the collective vision and expertise of the team.

In all cases, it is important to tailor the tone, level of detail, and emphasis of your business plan to resonate with the specific preferences and expectations of your audience. Be mindful of using jargon or technical terms that may not be familiar to all readers and provide clear explanations and context where necessary. Consider using visual aids, such as charts, graphs, and infographics, to enhance understanding and engagement. Ultimately, by customizing your business plan to address the needs and interests of investors, lenders, and internal stakeholders, you can increase the relevance, impact, and effectiveness of your strategic document.

Chapter 2

Research and Analysis

Market Research

Market research is a critical component of any business plan as it provides valuable insights into the market environment in which a company operates. By understanding the market and its dynamics, businesses can make informed decisions, identify opportunities, and develop effective strategies to reach their target customers. In this section, we will explore various techniques for conducting market research to gain a deeper understanding of your market and competition.

1. Primary Research: This involves gathering data directly from the source. Methods of primary research include surveys, focus groups, interviews, and observations. Surveys can be conducted online, over the phone, or in person to collect information from a sample of the target market. Focus groups bring together a small group of individuals to discuss specific topics related to the market. Interviews with industry experts, customers, or stakeholders can provide valuable insights into market trends and preferences.

2. Secondary Research: Secondary research involves gathering data that has already been collected and analyzed by other sources. This can include industry reports, market studies, government publications, and academic research. By reviewing existing data, businesses can gain a broader perspective on market trends, competitor strategies, and consumer behavior.

3. Competitor Analysis: Analyzing competitors is an essential part of market research. By identifying key competitors, businesses can assess their strengths and weaknesses, product offerings, pricing strategies, and market positioning.

This analysis helps businesses understand the competitive landscape and identify opportunities to differentiate themselves in the market.

4. Market Segmentation: Market segmentation involves dividing the market into distinct groups based on demographics, psychographics, behavior, or other factors. By segmenting the market, businesses can target specific customer segments with tailored marketing strategies and product offerings. Understanding the needs and preferences of different market segments can help businesses better serve their customers and gain a competitive advantage.

5. Trend Analysis: Monitoring market trends is crucial for staying ahead of the curve and identifying emerging opportunities. By tracking industry trends, technological advancements, consumer preferences, and regulatory changes, businesses can adapt their strategies to capitalize on new opportunities and mitigate risks.

6. SWOT Analysis: Conducting a SWOT analysis (Strengths, Weaknesses, Opportunities, Threats) helps businesses assess internal capabilities and external factors that may impact their competitiveness. By identifying strengths that can be leveraged, weaknesses that need to be addressed, opportunities for growth, and threats to be mitigated, businesses can develop strategies to capitalize on their strengths and overcome potential challenges.

7. Customer Feedback: Gathering feedback from customers through surveys, focus groups, or social media can provide valuable insights into customer preferences, satisfaction levels, and areas for improvement. By listening to customer feedback, businesses can tailor their products and services to meet customer needs and enhance customer satisfaction.

In conclusion, market research is a vital component of a business plan as it helps businesses understand their market, competition, and target customers. By employing various techniques such as primary and secondary research, competitor analysis, market segmentation, trend analysis, SWOT analysis, and customer feedback, businesses can gather valuable insights to make informed decisions and develop effective strategies to drive success in the market. Conducting thorough market research is essential for businesses to stay competitive, identify growth opportunities, and meet the evolving needs of their customers.

Industry Analysis

Industry analysis is a crucial component of any business plan as it provides valuable insights into the external factors that can impact your business's success. By understanding the industry in which your business operates, you can make informed decisions, identify opportunities for growth, and mitigate potential risks. In this section, we will delve into the importance of industry analysis, the key components to consider, and some strategies for conducting a comprehensive analysis.

Importance of Industry Analysis

Industry analysis helps you gain a deeper understanding of the market dynamics, competitive landscape, and trends that shape the industry. By staying informed about industry trends and developments, you can anticipate changes, capitalize on emerging opportunities, and stay ahead of the competition. Industry analysis also enables you to identify potential threats and challenges that may impact your business, allowing you to proactively devise strategies to address them.

Key Components of Industry Analysis

1. Market Size and Growth: Evaluate the size of the market in which your business operates and forecast its growth potential. Understanding market trends and growth projections can help you assess the demand for your products or services and plan for expansion opportunities.

2. Competitive Landscape: Identify key competitors in your industry, their market share, strengths, weaknesses, and strategies. Analyzing competitors can help you position your business effectively, differentiate your offerings, and identify areas for competitive advantage.

3. Regulatory Environment: Understand the regulatory landscape governing your industry, including licensing requirements, compliance standards, and any upcoming regulatory changes. Compliance with regulations is crucial for ensuring the sustainability and legality of your business operations.

4. Technological Trends: Stay abreast of technological advancements and innovations that are shaping the industry. Assess how technology is disrupting traditional business models, creating new opportunities, and changing consumer behavior. Leveraging technology can give your business a competitive edge and drive innovation.

5. Consumer Behavior: Analyze consumer preferences, buying patterns, and demographics within your industry. Understanding consumer behavior can help you tailor your products or services to meet customer needs, improve marketing strategies, and enhance customer satisfaction.

Strategies for Conducting Industry Analysis

1. Primary Research: Conduct surveys, interviews, or focus groups with industry experts, customers, and stakeholders to gather firsthand insights into market trends and challenges.

2. Secondary Research: Utilize industry reports, market studies, government publications, and trade publications to gather data and information on industry trends, forecasts, and competitive analysis.

3. SWOT Analysis: Conduct a SWOT analysis (Strengths, Weaknesses, Opportunities, and Threats) to assess your business's internal capabilities and external factors influencing your industry. This analysis can help you identify strategic priorities and areas for improvement.

4. Networking: Attend industry events, conferences, and networking sessions to connect with industry professionals, stay updated on industry trends, and gather valuable insights from peers and experts.

In conclusion, industry analysis is a critical aspect of developing a comprehensive business plan. By thoroughly examining industry trends, insights, and competitive factors, you can position your business for success, capitalize on opportunities, and navigate challenges effectively. Stay vigilant, adapt to changes, and leverage industry analysis to drive strategic decision-making and sustainable growth.

Customer Analysis

Customer Analysis is a crucial aspect of any business plan as it provides valuable insights into the target market and helps in creating effective marketing strategies. By understanding the needs, preferences, behaviors, and demographics of your potential customers, you can tailor your products or services to meet their specific requirements. In this section, we will delve deeper into the process of defining your target market and creating customer personas.

Defining your target market involves identifying the specific group of people or businesses that are most likely to purchase your products or services. This can be based on factors such as age, gender, income level, location, interests, and buying behavior. By narrowing down your target market, you can focus your marketing efforts and resources on reaching those who are most likely to convert into loyal customers.

Creating customer personas goes a step further by developing detailed profiles of your ideal customers. These personas are fictional representations of your target customers, based on real data and research. Each persona should include information such as demographics, psychographics, needs, pain points, goals, and preferences. By humanizing your target audience through personas, you can better understand their motivations and tailor your marketing messages and offerings to resonate with them.

When creating customer personas, it is essential to gather information through various research methods such as surveys, interviews, and market analysis. You can also utilize data from existing customers, social media insights, and industry reports to paint a comprehensive picture of your target audience. By understanding the motivations, challenges, and aspirations of your customers, you can develop products or services that address their specific needs and create personalized marketing campaigns that resonate with them.

Moreover, customer personas help in guiding product development, pricing strategies, messaging, and distribution channels. They also enable you to anticipate customer behaviors, preferences, and trends, allowing you to stay ahead of the competition and adapt quickly to changing market dynamics. By continuously refining and updating your customer personas based on feedback and data analysis, you can ensure that your business remains relevant and customer-centric.

In conclusion, customer analysis is a fundamental aspect of a business plan that provides valuable insights into the target market and helps in creating effective marketing strategies. By defining your target market and creating detailed customer personas, you can better understand your customers' needs, preferences, and behaviors, and tailor your products or services to meet their specific requirements. Customer personas serve as a valuable tool for guiding strategic decision-making, fostering customer engagement, and driving business growth.

SWOT Analysis

SWOT analysis is a strategic planning tool utilized by businesses to identify internal strengths and weaknesses, as well as external opportunities and threats. By conducting a SWOT analysis, businesses can gain valuable insights that help shape their business strategies and decision-making processes. Let's delve deeper into each component of a SWOT analysis:

Strengths:

Strengths are internal factors that give a business a competitive advantage and contribute to its success. These can include aspects such as a strong brand reputation, unique products or services, talented workforce, efficient operations, loyal customer base, or proprietary technology. Identifying and leveraging strengths allows a business to capitalize on its core competencies and differentiate itself from competitors.

Weaknesses:

Weaknesses are internal factors that hinder a business's performance and limit its growth potential. These may include factors such as inadequate resources, outdated technology, poor management, lack of brand recognition, or high employee turnover. By recognizing weaknesses, businesses can develop strategies to address and mitigate these challenges, ultimately improving their overall performance and competitiveness.

Opportunities:

Opportunities are external factors in the business environment that can be leveraged to enhance growth and profitability. These can include market trends, industry developments, emerging technologies, changing consumer preferences, or new business partnerships. Identifying and capitalizing on opportunities enables businesses to expand their market reach, drive innovation, and stay ahead of the competition.

Threats:

Threats are external factors that pose risks and challenges to a business's success. These may include factors such as economic downturns, increased competition, regulatory changes, shifting consumer behavior, or technological disruptions. By identifying threats, businesses can develop contingency plans and strategies to mitigate risks, safeguard their operations, and adapt to changing circumstances effectively.

Conducting a SWOT analysis involves gathering relevant data, analyzing internal and external factors, and synthesizing the information to form actionable insights. It is essential to involve key stakeholders, such as management team members, employees, and industry experts, in the SWOT analysis process to ensure a comprehensive and well-rounded assessment.

Furthermore, businesses should regularly revisit and update their SWOT analysis to reflect changes in the business environment and ensure that their strategies remain aligned with current conditions. By incorporating the findings of a SWOT analysis into their business planning process, businesses can make informed decisions, capitalize on opportunities, mitigate risks, and drive sustainable growth and success.

Competitive Analysis

Competitive Analysis is a critical component of any business plan as it helps you understand your competitive landscape, identify potential threats and opportunities, and strategically position your business for success. In this section, we will delve into the importance of conducting a thorough competitive analysis and provide a step-by-step guide on how to analyze your competitors effectively.

Importance of Competitive Analysis:

Understanding your competitors is essential for several reasons:

1. Identifying Strengths and Weaknesses: By analyzing your competitors, you can uncover their strengths and weaknesses, which can help you capitalize on their weaknesses and differentiate your business based on your strengths.

2. Market Positioning: Competitive analysis allows you to position your business effectively in the market by identifying gaps in the market, understanding customer preferences, and differentiating your products or services from competitors.

3. Strategic Planning: By understanding your competitors' strategies, market share, and target audience, you can develop a strategic plan that leverages your competitive advantages and mitigates potential threats.

Steps to Conduct a Competitive Analysis:

1. Identify Your Competitors: Start by listing your direct and indirect competitors. Direct competitors offer similar products or services to the same target market, while indirect competitors may offer alternative solutions to the same customer problem.

2. Gather Information: Collect data on your competitors' products or services, pricing strategies, marketing tactics, target audience, distribution channels, and market share. Utilize sources such as their websites, social media profiles, annual reports, and industry reports.

3. SWOT Analysis: Conduct a SWOT analysis for each competitor to identify their strengths, weaknesses, opportunities, and threats. This will help you understand how your business can capitalize on their weaknesses and differentiate itself in the market.

4. Benchmarking: Compare your business performance metrics with those of your competitors to identify areas where you excel and where you may need to improve. This can include metrics such as market share, revenue growth, customer satisfaction, and brand awareness.

5. Positioning Strategy: Based on your competitive analysis, develop a positioning strategy that highlights your unique selling proposition (USP) and communicates how your business stands out from competitors. This will help you attract and retain customers in a competitive market.

6. Competitive Advantage: Identify your competitive advantage, whether it's through product innovation, superior customer service, pricing strategy, or brand reputation. Highlighting this advantage in your marketing and sales efforts can help you gain a competitive edge.

7. Monitoring and Adaptation: Competitive analysis is an ongoing process. Continuously monitor your competitors' activities, market trends, and customer feedback to adapt your strategies accordingly. Stay agile and be prepared to pivot based on changing market conditions.

By conducting a comprehensive competitive analysis and leveraging the insights gained, you can position your business effectively in the market, differentiate yourself from competitors, and create a sustainable competitive advantage. This strategic approach will not only help you attract customers and grow your business but also navigate challenges and seize opportunities in a competitive business environment.

Chapter 3

Executive Summary

Purpose of the Executive Summary

The executive summary is a critical component of a business plan as it serves as the first impression of your business to potential investors, lenders, and other stakeholders. In this 500-word detailed section, we will explore the purpose of the executive summary, why it is crucial, and how to craft an effective one.

Purpose of the Executive Summary

The executive summary is a concise overview of the key aspects of your business plan. Its primary purpose is to provide a snapshot of your business to busy readers who may not have the time to go through the entire document. The executive summary should grab the reader's attention, highlight the most important points of your business plan, and create interest in learning more about your business.

Why It's Crucial

1. First Impression: The executive summary is usually the first section of your business plan that readers will encounter. A well-crafted executive summary can captivate the reader's interest and encourage them to delve deeper into the details of your plan.

2. Decision-Making Tool: Investors and lenders often use the executive summary as a decision-making tool to quickly assess the viability and potential of your business. It helps them determine whether your business aligns with their investment criteria.

3. Communication Tool: The executive summary serves as a communication tool to convey your business concept, goals, and unique selling points in a clear and concise manner. It helps stakeholders understand the essence of your business without having to read through lengthy sections of the plan.

4. Summary of Key Information: By summarizing the essential elements of your business plan, the executive summary provides a comprehensive overview of your business model, market opportunity, financial projections, and funding requirements.

How to Craft an Effective Executive Summary

1. Start Strong: Begin the executive summary with a compelling opening that captures the reader's attention. Clearly state the purpose of your business and what sets it apart from competitors.

2. Summarize Key Points: Provide a brief overview of your business concept, mission, vision, objectives, market opportunity, and financial highlights. Highlight the most critical aspects of your business plan.

3. Be Concise: Keep the executive summary concise and to the point. Avoid unnecessary details and focus on presenting the most relevant information that showcases the potential of your business.

4. Use Clear Language: Use clear and straightforward language to ensure that the reader can easily understand the content. Avoid jargon or technical terms that may confuse the reader.

5. Showcase Your Unique Selling Proposition: Clearly articulate what makes your business unique and why customers will choose your products or services over competitors. Highlight your competitive advantage and value proposition.

6. Highlight Financial Projections: Provide a snapshot of your financial projections, including revenue forecasts, funding requirements, and expected profitability. This gives investors insight into the financial viability of your business.

7. End with a Call to Action: Conclude the executive summary with a strong call to action, inviting readers to further explore your business plan or schedule a meeting to discuss potential partnerships or investments.

In summary, the executive summary is a crucial part of a business plan that plays a significant role in shaping stakeholders' perceptions of your business. By crafting a compelling and informative executive summary, you can effectively communicate the essence of your business and generate interest in your venture.

Business Overview

The Business Overview section of a business plan serves as a crucial snapshot that encapsulates the essence of your business. It is the first impression that potential investors, lenders, and stakeholders will have of your company, making it essential to craft a clear and compelling narrative. This section provides an overview of your business concept, mission, and vision, outlining the core elements that define your organization's purpose and direction.

1. Business Concept:

The business concept is the fundamental idea behind your venture. It encapsulates what your business does, the problem it solves, and the value it offers to customers. In this section, you should clearly articulate the products or services you provide, the target market you serve, and the unique selling proposition that sets your offerings apart from competitors. By succinctly describing your business concept, you set the foundation for the rest of the business plan and establish a framework for strategic decision-making.

2. Mission Statement:

Your mission statement defines the purpose and values that drive your business. It articulates why your company exists, who it serves, and what principles guide its operations. A well-crafted mission statement should be concise, inspirational, and reflective of your core beliefs and aspirations. It serves as a compass that aligns your team members, customers, and stakeholders towards a common goal, fostering a sense of purpose and direction within the organization.

3. Vision Statement:

The vision statement outlines your long-term aspirations and goals for the future. It describes the desired state of your business and the impact you aim to achieve in the industry or market. A compelling vision statement should be ambitious, inspiring, and realistic, providing a roadmap for growth and expansion. By painting a vivid picture of what success looks like for your company, the vision statement motivates stakeholders to work towards a shared vision and sets the strategic trajectory for achieving your business objectives.

In summary, the Business Overview section of a business plan serves as a strategic compass that guides your organization towards success. By clearly articulating your business concept, mission, and vision, you establish a strong foundation for growth, innovation, and sustainability. This section should communicate the essence of your business in a concise and compelling manner, capturing the attention and interest of readers while setting the stage for the detailed analysis and planning that follows in the subsequent chapters of the business plan. Remember, a well-crafted Business Overview not only defines who you are as a business but also sets the tone for what you aim to achieve in the competitive landscape of the market.

Business Objectives

Business objectives are crucial elements of a business plan as they serve as the roadmap that guides the direction and focus of a company. By setting clear and specific objectives, businesses can establish measurable goals that help track progress, make informed decisions, and ultimately achieve success. In this section, we will delve deeper into outlining short-term and long-term goals within a business plan.

Short-term goals are typically achievable within a defined period, usually ranging from a few months to a year. These goals are often focused on immediate actions and outcomes that can propel the business forward in the short term. When outlining short-term goals in a business plan, it is important to ensure that they are specific, measurable, achievable, relevant, and time-bound (SMART). This means that each goal should be clearly defined, quantifiable, realistic, aligned with the overall business objectives, and have a set timeline for completion.

Examples of short-term goals that can be included in a business plan may involve increasing sales by a certain percentage, launching a new product or service, expanding into a new market segment, improving customer satisfaction ratings, enhancing brand awareness through marketing campaigns, or reducing operational costs through efficiency measures. These goals should be directly tied to the business's strategic priorities and contribute to its overall growth and success.

On the other hand, long-term goals are broader objectives that span over a more extended period, typically beyond one year. These goals provide a sense of direction and vision for the business, outlining where the company aims to be in the future and what it aspires to achieve in the long run. Long-term goals are instrumental in shaping the overall strategy and decision-making processes of a business.

When defining long-term goals in a business plan, it is essential to consider the overarching mission and vision of the company. Long-term goals should be ambitious yet attainable, setting the bar high for the business to strive towards continuous improvement and sustainable growth. These goals should also be aligned with the core values and strategic priorities of the business, driving organizational focus and cohesion.

Examples of long-term goals that can be included in a business plan may involve achieving a certain market share within a specific industry, becoming a market leader in a particular product category, expanding globally into new territories, developing innovative products or services that disrupt the market, increasing profitability and shareholder value, or establishing a strong brand presence that resonates with customers.

In conclusion, outlining short-term and long-term goals in a business plan is essential for setting a clear direction and defining the path to success for a company. By establishing specific and measurable objectives, businesses can create a roadmap that guides their actions, drives performance, and ultimately leads to achieving sustainable growth and profitability. Effective goal-setting within a business plan ensures that the business remains focused, motivated, and aligned towards realizing its vision and fulfilling its mission.

Market Opportunity

The market opportunity section of a business plan plays a crucial role in outlining the potential for success and growth within a specific market or industry. By conducting thorough research and analysis, you can identify key insights and opportunities that will guide your business strategy and decision-making processes. This section is essential for demonstrating to investors, lenders, and stakeholders the viability and potential for your business idea.

1. Market Size and Growth Trends:

Begin by providing an overview of the size and growth trends of the target market. This includes data on the total addressable market (TAM) and the projected growth rate. By understanding the market's size and growth potential, you can assess the scalability and long-term sustainability of your business.

2. Target Market Segmentation:

Segmenting the market allows you to identify specific customer groups with distinct needs and preferences. Define your target market segments based on demographics, psychographics, behavior, and other relevant criteria. This segmentation will help you tailor your products/services and marketing strategies to effectively reach and engage your target customers.

3. Customer Needs and Pain Points:

Delve into the needs, challenges, and pain points of your target customers. By understanding what drives their purchase decisions and how your offerings can address their problems or fulfill their desires, you can position your business as a solution provider that meets customer demands effectively.

4. Competitive Landscape Analysis:

Analyze the competitive landscape to identify existing players, their strengths and weaknesses, and the market share they hold. Assess how your business can differentiate itself from competitors and carve out a unique value proposition that resonates with customers. Understanding your competitive position will inform your market strategy and positioning efforts.

5. Market Trends and Opportunities:

Explore current and emerging trends in the market that present opportunities for growth and innovation. This could include technological advancements, shifting consumer preferences, regulatory changes, or industry disruptions. By staying ahead of trends and leveraging opportunities, you can position your business for sustained success and competitive advantage.

6. Market Entry Strategy:

Outline your approach to entering the market and capturing market share. This may involve tactics such as targeting a niche market segment, partnering with key stakeholders, leveraging strategic alliances, or implementing innovative marketing campaigns. Define your market entry strategy based on a deep understanding of the market dynamics and competitive landscape.

By highlighting key market insights and opportunities in your business plan, you demonstrate a thorough understanding of the market landscape and a strategic approach to capitalizing on growth prospects. This section serves as a roadmap for aligning your business goals with market realities, ultimately positioning your venture for success and sustainable growth in a competitive business environment.

Financial Highlights

The financial highlights section of a business plan serves as a crucial component that provides a concise overview of the financial health of the business, including key financial projections and funding requirements. This section is essential for investors, lenders, and stakeholders to quickly grasp the financial outlook of the business and assess its potential for success. Let's delve into the key elements typically included in the financial highlights section:

1. Financial Projections: This part of the financial highlights outlines the expected financial performance of the business over a specific period, usually three to five years. It includes projections for revenue, expenses, profits, and cash flow. These projections are based on thorough market research, industry analysis, and realistic assumptions about the business's growth trajectory.

2. Revenue Forecast: The revenue forecast details the expected income generated by the business through its products or services. It includes a breakdown of revenue streams, pricing strategies, sales volume projections, and any other sources of income. This projection is crucial for demonstrating the business's revenue-generating potential to investors and lenders.

3. Expense Projections: The expense projections outline the anticipated costs associated with running the business. This includes fixed costs (such as rent, utilities, salaries) and variable costs (such as materials, marketing expenses). By detailing the expected expenses, the business can demonstrate its ability to manage costs effectively and maintain profitability.

4. Profitability Analysis: The financial highlights section should include a profitability analysis that showcases the projected profits of the business. This analysis helps investors and lenders understand the potential return on investment and assess the overall financial viability of the business.

5. Cash Flow Forecast: Cash flow projections are crucial for assessing the business's ability to manage its finances effectively. This section outlines the expected cash inflows and outflows over a specific period, highlighting any potential cash flow constraints or opportunities for growth.

6. Funding Requirements: In this part of the financial highlights, the business outlines its funding needs to support its operations and growth plans. It details the amount of capital required, the purpose of the funding (such as working capital, expansion, or equipment purchases), and how the funds will be utilized to achieve the business's objectives.

7. Use of Funds: Alongside funding requirements, the financial highlights section should also include a breakdown of how the funds will be allocated. This provides transparency to investors and lenders on how their investment will be utilized and the expected outcomes from the capital infusion.

8. Financial Metrics: To provide a comprehensive snapshot of the business's financial health, key financial metrics such as return on investment (ROI), gross margin, break-even point, and debt-to-equity ratio may be included in this section. These metrics offer insights into the business's performance, profitability, and financial stability.

In conclusion, the financial highlights section of a business plan plays a vital role in showcasing the financial viability and growth potential of the business. By providing a snapshot of financial projections and funding requirements, this section enables investors, lenders, and stakeholders to assess the business's financial health and make informed decisions regarding investment or partnership opportunities. It is essential for entrepreneurs to carefully craft this section with accurate data, realistic projections, and a clear outline of the financial strategy to attract potential investors and support the business's long-term success.

Chapter 4

Company Description

Business Structure

Business Structure is a critical aspect of any business plan as it defines how your business is legally organized and operated. The choice of business structure can have significant implications on aspects such as liability, taxes, management control, and compliance requirements. Understanding the different types of business structures – sole proprietorship, limited liability company (LLC), and corporation – is essential for entrepreneurs to make informed decisions that align with their business goals and circumstances.

1. Sole Proprietorship:

A sole proprietorship is the simplest form of business structure and is owned and operated by a single individual. In this structure, there is no legal distinction between the owner and the business entity. The owner has full control over the business and retains all profits but is also personally liable for any debts or legal obligations of the business. Sole proprietorships are easy to set up, have minimal compliance requirements, and offer flexibility in decision-making.

2. Limited Liability Company (LLC):

An LLC is a popular business structure that combines the benefits of a corporation with the simplicity of a sole proprietorship. LLCs provide limited liability protection to owners, meaning their personal assets are separate from the business's liabilities. This shields owners from personal liability for the debts and actions of the business. LLCs offer flexibility in management structure and profit distribution, making them suitable for small to medium-sized businesses. Additionally, LLCs offer pass-through taxation, where profits and losses are reported on the owners' personal tax returns.

3. Corporation:

A corporation is a separate legal entity from its owners, known as shareholders. Corporations provide the highest level of liability protection, as shareholders are not personally liable for the company's debts or legal obligations. Corporations have a more complex structure with a board of directors, officers, and shareholders, and are subject to more regulatory requirements and formalities compared to other business structures. Corporations can issue stock and attract investment from shareholders, making them suitable for businesses looking to scale and raise capital.

Choosing the right business structure requires careful consideration of factors such as liability protection, tax implications, management control, and growth potential. Entrepreneurs should evaluate their business goals, risk tolerance, and long-term plans before selecting a business structure. Consulting with legal and financial professionals can provide valuable insights and guidance in making an informed decision.

In conclusion, understanding the nuances of different business structures is crucial for entrepreneurs embarking on their business ventures. Each structure has its own advantages and considerations, and the choice of business structure should align with the specific needs and objectives of the business. By selecting the appropriate business structure, entrepreneurs can establish a solid foundation for their operations, protect their interests, and position their business for growth and success in the long run.

Mission and Vision Statements

Mission and Vision Statements are essential components of a business plan as they articulate the purpose and direction of the organization. Crafting clear and inspiring statements helps define the identity of the business, guiding its strategic decisions and operations. In this section, we will delve into the importance of Mission and Vision Statements, how to differentiate between the two, and provide guidelines for creating impactful statements.

Importance of Mission and Vision Statements:

Mission and Vision Statements serve distinct purposes in a business plan. The Mission Statement outlines the fundamental purpose of the organization, including its core values, target customers, and primary objectives. It answers the question, "Why does this business exist?" On the other hand, the Vision Statement paints a picture of what the organization aspires to achieve in the future. It reflects the long-term goals and aspirations of the business, inspiring stakeholders and guiding strategic decision-making.

Crafting a Mission Statement:

1. Define Your Core Values: Start by identifying the fundamental beliefs and principles that drive your business. These values should align with the core purpose of the organization and guide its actions and decisions.

2. Identify Your Target Audience: Clearly define who your customers are and how your products or services meet their needs. Understanding your target market helps shape your mission statement to resonate with your audience.

3. Articulate Your Purpose: Clearly state the reason for your business's existence. What problem are you solving, and how are you making a difference in the market or community? Your mission statement should be concise, impactful, and memorable.

4. Ensure Alignment with Business Objectives: Your mission statement should align with the overall goals of the business plan. It should provide a sense of direction and purpose that guides all activities within the organization.

Crafting a Vision Statement:

1. Envision the Future: Imagine where you see your business in the long term. What impact do you want to make, and what success looks like for your organization? Your vision statement should be aspirational and inspirational.

2. Set Clear Goals: Outline specific, measurable goals that your business aims to achieve in the future. These goals should be ambitious yet realistic, providing a roadmap for the growth and development of the organization.

3. Reflect Your Values and Culture: Your vision statement should reflect the values and culture of your organization. It should inspire employees, customers, and other stakeholders to align their efforts towards a common goal.

4. Communicate Effectively: Ensure that your vision statement is clear, concise, and easily understood by all stakeholders. It should be memorable and evoke a sense of purpose and direction for the organization.

Differentiating Between Mission and Vision Statements:
While Mission and Vision Statements are closely related, they serve different purposes. The Mission Statement focuses on the present state of the organization, its purpose, and values. In contrast, the Vision Statement looks to the future, outlining the desired long-term goals and aspirations of the business. Together, these statements provide a comprehensive overview of the organization's identity, purpose, and direction.

Crafting clear and inspiring Mission and Vision Statements is a critical step in developing a comprehensive business plan. These statements not only define the purpose and direction of the organization but also serve as a guiding light for strategic decision-making and goal setting. By following the guidelines outlined above, business owners can create impactful statements that resonate with stakeholders and drive the success of their ventures.

Business Model
The business model is a crucial component of any business plan as it outlines how a company operates and generates revenue. A well-defined business model clarifies the fundamental logic of how a business creates, delivers, and captures

value. It is essential for entrepreneurs and stakeholders to understand the intricacies of their business model to ensure long-term success and sustainability.

1. Describing Your Business Operations:

- Start by providing a comprehensive description of your business operations. Explain the core activities involved in delivering your products or services to customers. This can include manufacturing processes, service delivery methods, supply chain logistics, and any other operational aspects that are critical to your business.

2. Revenue Streams:

- Clearly outline how your business generates revenue. Identify the primary sources of income, whether through product sales, service fees, subscription models, licensing agreements, or any other revenue streams. It's important to detail the pricing strategy for your offerings and how it aligns with your target market's willingness to pay.

3. Value Proposition:

- Define what sets your business apart from competitors and why customers should choose your products or services. Your value proposition should clearly articulate the unique benefits and value that customers will receive by engaging with your business. This is closely tied to how you position your offerings in the market and the problem they solve for your target audience.

4. Cost Structure:

- Discuss the costs associated with running your business. This includes both fixed and variable costs such as production expenses, overhead costs, marketing budgets, employee salaries, and any other expenditures necessary to operate the business. Understanding your cost structure is essential for pricing decisions and ensuring profitability.

5. Distribution Channels:

- Explain how your products or services reach customers. Detail the distribution channels you use to deliver value, whether through direct sales, online platforms, retail partnerships, or other distribution methods. Understanding your distribution strategy is crucial for reaching your target market effectively and efficiently.

6. Customer Relationships:

- Describe how you engage with customers to build lasting relationships and drive repeat business. This can include customer service initiatives, loyalty programs, feedback mechanisms, and other strategies to enhance customer satisfaction and retention. Strong customer relationships are key to long-term success and sustainable growth.

7. Key Partnerships:

- Identify any strategic partnerships or collaborations that are integral to your business model. This could involve suppliers, manufacturers, distribution partners, or other key stakeholders that contribute to the value chain of your business. Building strong partnerships can enhance operational efficiency and create new opportunities for growth.

8. Revenue Model:

- Summarize your overall revenue model, including how you plan to scale revenue generation over time. This could involve expanding into new markets, introducing new products or services, upselling to existing customers, or diversifying revenue streams. Articulate a clear path to sustainable revenue growth and profitability.

In conclusion, a well-crafted business model provides a roadmap for how a company operates, creates value for customers, and generates revenue. By understanding the key components of your business model and how they interconnect, you can make informed decisions that drive business success and strategic growth. It is essential to regularly review and refine your business model to adapt to changing market conditions and ensure long-term viability in a competitive landscape.

Location and Facilities

Choosing the right location for your business can have a significant impact on its success. The physical location of your business can affect customer traffic, accessibility, visibility, and operational efficiency. In this section of your business plan, you will outline the details about your business's physical location and facilities to provide a clear understanding of where your business will be situated and how it will operate.

1. Business Location:

Describe the specific address or geographical area where your business will be located. Provide details on the proximity to major roads, public transportation, parking availability, and any neighboring businesses or amenities. Consider factors such as target market demographics, foot traffic, and competition in the area.

2. Facilities Description:

Outline the physical space where your business will operate, including the size, layout, and design of the facilities. Specify whether you will lease, rent, or own the space. Discuss any renovations or modifications needed to accommodate your business operations. Include details about the amenities, utilities, and infrastructure available at the location.

3. Accessibility and Convenience:

Explain how easily customers, suppliers, and employees can access your business location. Consider factors such as proximity to major highways, public transportation options, parking facilities, and ADA compliance for individuals with disabilities. Highlight any advantages or challenges associated with the location in terms of accessibility.

4. Zoning and Regulations:

Address any zoning regulations, permits, or licenses required for operating your business at the chosen location. Ensure compliance with local, state, and federal regulations regarding land use, building codes, health and safety standards, and environmental considerations. Discuss how you will navigate regulatory requirements to establish and maintain your business legally.

5. Security and Safety Measures:

Discuss the security measures in place to protect your business premises, assets, and personnel. Include details about surveillance systems, alarm systems, access control measures, and emergency response protocols. Prioritize the safety of employees and customers by outlining procedures for handling emergencies, accidents, or security threats.

6. Expansion and Growth Potential:

Evaluate the scalability and growth potential of your chosen location and facilities. Consider whether the space can accommodate future expansion, additional services, or increased production capacity as your business grows. Outline any plans for scaling up or relocating based on market demand and business growth projections.

7. Contingency Plans:

Develop contingency plans for unforeseen events or disruptions that could impact your business location and facilities. Consider risks such as natural disasters, utility outages, or economic downturns and outline strategies for mitigating these risks. Identify backup locations or alternative facilities to ensure business continuity in case of emergencies.

In conclusion, providing detailed information about your business's physical location and facilities in your business plan demonstrates your thorough understanding of the operational requirements and strategic considerations involved in establishing and maintaining a successful business. By carefully planning and evaluating the location and facilities aspects of your business, you

49

can optimize efficiency, attract customers, and create a safe and conducive environment for business operations.

Legal Considerations

When creating a business plan, it is crucial to address the legal considerations that govern your business operations. From choosing the appropriate legal structure to obtaining the necessary licenses and permits, understanding and complying with legal requirements is essential for the success and sustainability of your business. In this section, we will delve into the key aspects of legal considerations that should be outlined in your business plan.

1. Legal Structure:

The legal structure of your business defines how it is organized and operated in the eyes of the law. Common legal structures include sole proprietorship, partnership, limited liability company (LLC), and corporation. Each structure has its own implications in terms of liability, taxation, and governance. It is important to clearly define the legal structure of your business in your business plan to provide clarity on how your business will be managed and how profits will be distributed among owners.

2. Licenses and Permits:

Depending on the nature of your business and its location, you may be required to obtain certain licenses and permits to operate legally. These could include general business licenses, industry-specific permits, health and safety certifications, and zoning approvals. It is essential to research and identify all the necessary licenses and permits that apply to your business and include them in your business plan. Demonstrating compliance with legal requirements instills confidence in stakeholders and helps avoid potential legal issues in the future.

3. Intellectual Property Protection:

If your business involves unique products, services, or inventions, it is important to consider intellectual property protection. This could include patents for inventions, trademarks for brand names and logos, and copyrights for creative

50

works. Protecting your intellectual property assets can safeguard your competitive advantage and prevent others from infringing on your rights. Including a section on intellectual property in your business plan demonstrates your commitment to protecting your innovations and assets.

4. Contracts and Agreements:
Contracts play a vital role in defining the relationships and obligations of your business with customers, suppliers, employees, and partners. It is advisable to outline key contracts and agreements that are essential for your business operations in your business plan. This could include customer agreements, supplier contracts, employment agreements, and partnership agreements. Clearly defining the terms and conditions of these agreements can help mitigate risks and disputes in the future.

5. Compliance and Regulatory Requirements:
Businesses are subject to a wide range of laws and regulations at the local, state, and federal levels. Ensuring compliance with these requirements is crucial to avoid penalties, fines, and legal sanctions. Your business plan should address how your business will adhere to relevant laws and regulations, such as labor laws, environmental regulations, data protection laws, and industry-specific standards. Demonstrating a commitment to legal compliance in your business plan showcases your ethical standards and risk management practices.

In conclusion, addressing legal considerations in your business plan is essential for establishing a solid foundation for your business. By clearly outlining the legal structure, licenses and permits, intellectual property protection, contracts and agreements, and compliance with regulatory requirements, you demonstrate a proactive approach to legal compliance and risk management. This not only instills confidence in stakeholders but also helps protect your business from potential legal challenges. By integrating legal considerations into your business plan, you set the stage for a successful and sustainable business venture.

Chapter 5

Products or Services

Product or Service Description

The Products or Services section of your business plan is crucial as it provides a detailed overview of what you offer to your target market. This section plays a significant role in showcasing the value proposition of your business and how your offerings meet the needs and demands of your customers.

Product or Service Description:

In this part of the business plan, you need to provide a comprehensive description of the products or services that your business offers. It should include details such as the features, benefits, and specifications of each product or service. Be sure to clearly articulate how your offerings solve a problem or fulfill a need for your target customers.

For products, describe the physical attributes, design, and functionality. Highlight any unique or innovative features that set your products apart from competitors. Include information about the materials used, manufacturing process, and any relevant patents or trademarks.

When describing services, outline the specific offerings, processes, and methodologies that differentiate your services from others in the market. Explain how your services are delivered, the expertise of your team, and any specialized skills or qualifications that give you a competitive edge.

Unique Selling Proposition (USP):

Your Unique Selling Proposition (USP) is what differentiates your products or services from those of your competitors and gives you a competitive advantage.

Clearly identify and articulate what makes your offerings unique and why customers should choose your business over others.

Your USP could be based on factors such as superior quality, innovative features, competitive pricing, exceptional customer service, niche specialization, or sustainable practices. It is essential to communicate your USP effectively to your target audience to attract and retain customers.

Development Stage:
Provide an overview of the current status of your products or services, including whether they are in the conceptual, development, testing, or market-ready stage. Discuss any future development plans or enhancements that are in the pipeline to keep your offerings relevant and competitive in the market.

Pricing Strategy:
Outline your pricing strategy for your products or services, including the rationale behind your pricing decisions. Factors to consider when setting prices may include production costs, competitor pricing, perceived value to customers, and profit margins. Explain any discounts, promotions, or bundling strategies you plan to implement to attract customers.

Intellectual Property:
If applicable, discuss any intellectual property rights associated with your products or services, such as patents, trademarks, or copyrights. Highlight how these protections safeguard your innovations and creations from being copied or imitated by competitors. Intellectual property can add value to your business and create barriers to entry for competitors.

In conclusion, the Products or Services section of your business plan is essential for clearly defining what your business offers, how it stands out in the market, and how it meets the needs of your target customers. By presenting a detailed and compelling description of your products or services, you can effectively communicate the value proposition of your business and attract potential investors, partners, and customers.

Unique Selling Proposition (USP)

The Unique Selling Proposition (USP) is a critical component of a business plan that helps differentiate your products or services from competitors in the market. It serves as the foundation for your marketing and sales strategies, helping you communicate the value you offer to your target audience. In this section, we will delve deeper into understanding the concept of USP and how to effectively identify what sets your offerings apart.

Understanding the Unique Selling Proposition (USP):

The Unique Selling Proposition (USP) is a statement that defines what makes your products or services unique and valuable to customers. It highlights the specific benefits or advantages that set your offerings apart from competitors. A strong USP is essential for attracting and retaining customers, as it helps create a strong brand identity and resonates with your target market.

Identifying Your USP:

1. Know Your Audience: Understand the needs, preferences, and pain points of your target customers. Identify what matters most to them and how your offerings can address their challenges or fulfill their desires.

2. Competitive Analysis: Conduct a thorough analysis of your competitors to identify gaps in the market and opportunities for differentiation. Determine what your competitors are offering and how you can position your products or services uniquely.

3. Highlight Your Strengths: Identify your core strengths, whether it's superior quality, innovative features, exceptional customer service, or competitive pricing. Focus on what sets your business apart and resonates with your target audience.

4. Value Proposition: Clearly articulate the value that your offerings provide to customers. How does your product or service solve a problem, meet a need, or enhance the lives of your customers? Communicate this value proposition effectively in your USP.

5. Emphasize Benefits: Instead of simply listing features, emphasize the benefits that customers will experience by choosing your products or services. How will your offerings improve their lives, save them time or money, or fulfill their aspirations?

6. Crafting Your USP: Once you have identified what sets your offerings apart, distill this information into a concise and compelling USP. Your USP should be clear, concise, and memorable, capturing the essence of what makes your business unique.

Communicating Your USP:

1. Consistent Messaging: Integrate your USP into all your marketing and communication efforts to ensure a consistent brand message. Your USP should resonate across your website, advertising campaigns, social media, and customer interactions.

2. Differentiation Strategy: Use your USP as a strategic tool to position your business in the market. Emphasize your unique strengths and advantages to create a competitive edge and attract your target customers.

3. Testing and Refinement: Continuously test and refine your USP based on customer feedback, market trends, and competitive dynamics. Adapt your USP as needed to stay relevant and compelling in the eyes of your target audience.

In conclusion, a well-defined Unique Selling Proposition (USP) is a powerful tool for differentiating your business in a competitive market landscape. By identifying what sets your offerings apart and communicating this uniqueness effectively, you can attract and retain customers, build a strong brand identity, and drive business growth. Invest time and effort in crafting a compelling USP that resonates with your target audience and positions your business for success.

Development Stage

In the chapter on Products or Services within a business plan, a crucial aspect to address is the Development Stage of your offerings. This section provides a detailed overview of the current status of your products or services, as well as outlining your future development plans. By clearly articulating where your products/services stand in terms of development and what the roadmap looks like moving forward, you demonstrate to potential investors, lenders, and stakeholders that you have a clear vision for the growth and evolution of your business.

When discussing the current status of your products/services, it is important to provide a comprehensive description of what you offer. This includes detailing the features, functionality, and benefits of your offerings. By clearly articulating the unique value proposition of your products/services, you can differentiate yourself from competitors and showcase why customers should choose your offerings over others in the market.

Furthermore, in the Development Stage section, you should outline any milestones or achievements that have been reached thus far. This could include product launches, successful pilot tests, or key partnerships that have been established. By highlighting these accomplishments, you build credibility and instill confidence in the viability of your products/services.

In addition to discussing the current status, it is essential to provide insight into your future development plans. This involves outlining your product roadmap and detailing how you plan to enhance or expand your offerings over time. Whether it involves introducing new features, entering new markets, or launching complementary products/services, painting a clear picture of your growth strategy is crucial for demonstrating the scalability and sustainability of your business.

Moreover, discussing your future development plans also entails addressing any challenges or risks that may impact the execution of your strategy. By acknowledging potential obstacles and outlining contingency plans, you showcase your preparedness and ability to adapt to changing market conditions.

It is equally important to highlight any intellectual property considerations related to your products/services in this section. This could include discussing patents, trademarks, copyrights, or any other forms of intellectual property protection that are relevant to your offerings. By demonstrating that you have taken steps to safeguard your innovations, you provide assurance to investors and stakeholders regarding the long-term viability and competitiveness of your products/services.

In conclusion, the Development Stage section of your business plan is a critical component that showcases your current progress, future growth plans, and intellectual property considerations related to your products/services. By effectively communicating your vision for product/service development, you set the foundation for building confidence and support for your business among potential investors and stakeholders.

Pricing Strategy

Pricing strategy is a crucial aspect of a business plan as it directly impacts your revenue, profit margins, and overall competitiveness in the market. Setting the right price for your products or services requires a deep understanding of your target market, competition, costs, and value proposition. In this section, we will delve into the key considerations for developing an effective pricing strategy and why it is essential for the success of your business.

1. Understanding the Market:

Before determining the price for your offerings, it is imperative to conduct thorough market research to understand the pricing dynamics in your industry. Analyze your competitors' pricing strategies, customer preferences, and willingness to pay. Identify the pricing range in the market and assess where your product or service stands in terms of quality, features, and value proposition.

2. Cost Analysis:

Calculate all the costs associated with producing and delivering your products or services. This includes direct costs like materials, labor, and overhead expenses. Understanding your cost structure is crucial in setting a price that covers your expenses while ensuring profitability. Consider both variable and fixed costs to determine a pricing strategy that allows you to achieve your desired profit margins.

3. Value-Based Pricing:

One effective pricing strategy is value-based pricing, where the price is determined by the perceived value of your offerings to customers. Consider the unique benefits and features of your products or services that differentiate them from competitors. Price your offerings based on the value they provide to customers rather than solely on costs. Communicate the value proposition effectively to justify the price to customers.

4. Competitive Pricing:

Competitive pricing involves setting prices based on what your competitors are charging for similar products or services. This strategy requires monitoring the market closely and adjusting your prices to stay competitive. While competitive pricing can help attract price-sensitive customers, it is essential to differentiate your offerings through quality, service, or branding to justify any premium pricing.

5. Pricing Strategies:
There are various pricing strategies you can consider based on your business goals and market positioning. These include penetration pricing, where you set a low initial price to gain market share, and then gradually increase prices. Price skimming involves setting high prices initially to target early adopters and then lowering prices over time. Subscription pricing, freemium models, and dynamic pricing are other strategies to explore based on your business model.

6. Promotional Pricing:
Promotional pricing tactics such as discounts, bundle offers, and seasonal promotions can be used to attract customers, drive sales, and create a sense of urgency. However, it is important to carefully plan and execute promotional pricing to avoid devaluing your products or eroding your profit margins in the long run.

In conclusion, pricing strategy is a critical component of your business plan that directly impacts your revenue and profitability. By understanding your market, costs, value proposition, and competition, you can develop a pricing strategy that maximizes revenue and sustains your business growth. Careful consideration of pricing factors and regular monitoring of market trends will help you adapt your pricing strategy to meet the evolving needs of your customers and maintain a competitive edge in the market.

Intellectual Property
Intellectual property (IP) is a crucial aspect of any business plan, as it protects your unique ideas, inventions, and creations from being used or copied by others

without your permission. Understanding and safeguarding your intellectual property rights can provide a competitive advantage, enhance your business's value, and prevent unauthorized use of your innovations. In this section, we will discuss the different types of intellectual property – patents, trademarks, and copyrights – and how they can be utilized to protect your business assets.

Patents: A patent is a form of intellectual property that grants the inventor exclusive rights to their invention for a limited period, typically 20 years from the filing date. Patents can cover products, processes, or designs that are new, non-obvious, and useful. By obtaining a patent, you can prevent others from making, using, selling, or importing your invention without your permission. It is essential to conduct a thorough patent search to ensure that your invention is novel and not already protected by existing patents. Including information about any patents you hold or are in the process of obtaining in your business plan can demonstrate the uniqueness and innovation of your products or services.

Trademarks: A trademark is a recognizable sign, design, or expression that distinguishes your goods or services from those of others in the market. It can be a word, logo, slogan, or combination thereof that identifies your brand and builds customer loyalty. Registering a trademark provides exclusive rights to use that mark in connection with your products or services and protects against unauthorized use by competitors. Including details about your registered trademarks and branding strategies in your business plan can showcase your commitment to building a strong brand identity and customer recognition.

Copyrights: Copyright is a form of intellectual property that protects original works of authorship, such as literary, artistic, musical, or software creations. Copyright gives the creator the exclusive right to reproduce, distribute, perform, or display their work. Unlike patents and trademarks, copyright protection is automatic upon creation and registration is not required, although it can provide additional benefits in legal disputes. Including information about any copyrighted materials, such as software code, marketing materials, or creative content, in your business plan can demonstrate the value of your original creations and the steps taken to protect them.

Incorporating a comprehensive intellectual property strategy into your business plan can enhance your credibility with investors, partners, and stakeholders by demonstrating your commitment to protecting your innovations and brand assets. It is essential to consult with intellectual property professionals, such as patent attorneys or trademark agents, to ensure that your IP rights are adequately secured and enforced. By proactively managing your intellectual property portfolio, you can safeguard your competitive advantage, mitigate risks of infringement, and maximize the value of your intangible assets in the marketplace.

In conclusion, understanding the importance of patents, trademarks, and copyrights in protecting your intellectual property is essential for long-term business success. By incorporating a robust IP strategy into your business plan, you can establish a solid foundation for growth, innovation, and differentiation in the market. Remember that intellectual property is a valuable asset that should be managed strategically and proactively to safeguard your business's future.

Chapter 6

Market Strategy

Marketing Plan

The marketing plan is a crucial component of your business plan as it outlines how you will promote and sell your products or services to your target customers. A well-crafted marketing plan helps you attract and retain customers, differentiate your business from competitors, and drive revenue growth. In this section, we will delve into the key elements of a marketing plan, including marketing strategies, branding, sales tactics, customer acquisition, and advertising and promotion.

Marketing Strategies:

Your marketing plan should detail the strategies you will use to reach and engage your target audience. This includes defining your target market segments, identifying their needs and preferences, and determining the most effective channels to reach them. Your marketing strategies may include online marketing tactics such as social media, content marketing, search engine optimization (SEO), email marketing, and pay-per-click advertising, as well as offline strategies like print ads, direct mail, events, and partnerships.

Branding:

Branding plays a vital role in establishing your business's identity and communicating its value proposition to customers. Your branding strategy should encompass your business name, logo, tagline, and messaging to create a consistent and compelling brand image. By defining your brand identity, you can differentiate your business from competitors, build trust and loyalty with customers, and increase brand awareness in the marketplace.

Sales Strategy:

Your sales strategy outlines how you will generate revenue by converting leads into customers. This includes defining your sales process, setting sales targets, and determining the roles and responsibilities of your sales team. Your sales strategy should address key aspects such as lead generation, lead nurturing, closing sales, upselling and cross-selling, and customer relationship management to maximize sales effectiveness and drive business growth.

Customer Acquisition:

Acquiring new customers is essential for business growth and sustainability. Your marketing plan should include strategies for attracting and retaining customers, such as offering promotions, discounts, referral programs, loyalty rewards, and exceptional customer service. By understanding your target customers' needs and preferences, you can tailor your customer acquisition strategies to effectively engage and convert prospects into loyal customers.

Advertising and Promotion:

Advertising and promotion tactics are essential for raising awareness of your business and driving customer engagement. Your marketing plan should outline the various channels and methods you will use to promote your products or services, such as online ads, social media campaigns, influencer partnerships, public relations efforts, and event sponsorships. By leveraging a mix of paid, earned, and owned media, you can maximize your reach and impact in the marketplace.

In conclusion, a well-developed marketing plan is essential for effectively promoting your products or services, attracting customers, and driving revenue growth. By outlining your marketing and sales strategies, branding efforts, customer acquisition tactics, and advertising and promotion initiatives, you can create a comprehensive roadmap for achieving your business objectives and establishing a strong market presence. Remember to regularly monitor and evaluate the performance of your marketing plan to make adjustments and optimize your strategies for continued success.

Branding

Branding is a critical aspect of any business plan as it defines your company's identity and sets you apart from competitors. It encompasses not just your logo and name, but also your messaging, values, and customer perception. In this chapter, we will delve into the importance of branding and how to effectively define your brand identity.

1. Importance of Branding:

Branding is more than just a logo or a catchy tagline. It is the essence of your business, encapsulating what you stand for, your values, and how you want to be perceived in the market. A strong brand can create trust and loyalty among customers, differentiate you from competitors, and drive customer acquisition and retention.

2. Defining Your Brand Identity:

a. Name: Your business name is the first impression customers have of your brand. It should be memorable, easy to spell and pronounce, and reflective of your business values and offerings.

b. Logo: A visually appealing and well-designed logo is crucial for brand recognition. It should be unique, scalable, and versatile to be used across various marketing materials.

c. Messaging: Your brand's messaging includes your tagline, mission statement, and brand voice. It should communicate your value proposition, resonate with your target audience, and be consistent across all communication channels.

3. Brand Identity Components:

a. Visual Identity: This includes your logo, color palette, typography, and design elements that visually represent your brand.

b. Brand Voice: Your brand voice encompasses the tone, style, and language used in all communications. It should be aligned with your brand values and resonate with your target audience.

c. Brand Values: These are the core principles and beliefs that guide your business decisions and actions. Your brand values should be authentic and reflected in every aspect of your business.

4. Brand Strategy:

a. Brand Positioning: Define how you want your brand to be perceived in the market and how you differentiate yourself from competitors.

b. Target Audience: Understand your target customers' demographics, behaviors, and preferences to tailor your brand messaging and offerings.

c. Brand Guidelines: Create a brand style guide that outlines how your brand elements should be used consistently across all touchpoints.

5. Brand Building:

a. Consistency: Ensure that your brand identity is consistent across all customer touchpoints, from your website and social media to packaging and customer service.

b. Storytelling: Use storytelling to convey your brand's history, values, and unique selling points to create an emotional connection with customers.

c. Brand Experience: Create a positive and memorable brand experience for customers at every interaction point to build brand loyalty.

In conclusion, branding is a powerful tool that can drive business growth and success. By defining your brand identity clearly and consistently, you can establish a strong brand presence in the market, attract loyal customers, and differentiate yourself from competitors. Invest time and effort in crafting a compelling brand identity that resonates with your target audience and aligns with your business goals for long-term success.

Sales Strategy

A well-defined sales strategy is crucial for the success of any business. It outlines the processes and methods through which a company will generate revenue by selling its products or services. By detailing your sales process and distribution channels in your business plan, you provide a roadmap for how you will reach and convert customers, ultimately driving growth and profitability.

Sales Process:

The sales process refers to the series of steps that a customer goes through from the initial contact with your business to making a purchase. It is essential to clearly define each stage of the sales process to ensure a smooth and efficient customer journey. Some common steps in a sales process include:

1. Prospecting: Identifying and qualifying potential leads who have shown interest in your offerings.

2. Needs Assessment: Understanding the specific needs and pain points of the prospect to tailor your pitch accordingly.

3. Presentation: Demonstrating how your products or services can address the customer's needs and provide value.

4. Handling Objections: Addressing any concerns or objections the prospect may have to move them closer to a purchase decision.

5. Closing: Securing the sale by finalizing the terms and completing the transaction.

6. Follow-Up: Maintaining contact with the customer post-sale to ensure satisfaction and foster long-term relationships.

Distribution Channels:

Distribution channels are the pathways through which a company delivers its products or services to customers. Choosing the right distribution channels is critical to reaching your target market effectively and efficiently. Here are some common distribution channels to consider:

1. Direct Sales: Selling products or services directly to customers through your own sales team or website.

2. Retail Distribution: Partnering with retail stores to sell your products on their shelves.

3. Online Sales: Leveraging e-commerce platforms to reach a broader audience and facilitate online transactions.

4. Wholesale Distribution: Selling products to other businesses in bulk for resale.

5. Channel Partnerships: Collaborating with other businesses or resellers to expand your reach and access new markets.

6. Franchising: Allowing independent operators to use your business model and sell your products under your brand.

It is important to evaluate the pros and cons of each distribution channel based on factors such as cost, reach, control, and customer experience. A multi-channel approach that combines different distribution channels can help diversify your revenue streams and mitigate risks.

Key Considerations:

When detailing your sales strategy in your business plan, consider the following key factors:

1. Target Audience: Understand your target market's preferences, behaviors, and buying habits to tailor your sales process effectively.

2. Competitive Landscape: Analyze your competitors' sales strategies and identify opportunities to differentiate your offerings.

3. Sales Metrics: Define key performance indicators (KPIs) to track and measure the effectiveness of your sales process and distribution channels.

4. Scalability: Ensure that your sales strategy is scalable to accommodate business growth and expansion.

5. Training and Support: Invest in training programs and support resources for your sales team to enhance their skills and performance.

By detailing a comprehensive sales strategy that encompasses your sales process and distribution channels, you can position your business for success and sustainable growth in the competitive marketplace. It serves as a roadmap for acquiring customers, driving revenue, and building lasting relationships that are essential for long-term success.

Customer Acquisition

Customer acquisition is a critical aspect of any business plan, as it directly impacts the growth and sustainability of a company. This section focuses on outlining strategies for attracting and retaining customers effectively.

1. Identifying Target Audience: The first step in customer acquisition is defining and understanding your target market. Conduct thorough market research to identify the demographics, preferences, and behaviors of your potential customers. This will help tailor your marketing and sales strategies to resonate with your target audience.

2. Creating a Marketing Plan: Develop a comprehensive marketing plan that outlines how you will reach your target customers. Utilize a mix of online and offline marketing channels such as social media, email marketing, content marketing, search engine optimization (SEO), and traditional advertising to increase brand visibility and attract potential customers.

3. Utilizing Customer Relationship Management (CRM) Systems: Implement a CRM system to track customer interactions, manage leads, and personalize communication with customers. By understanding customer preferences and behaviors, you can tailor your offerings to meet their needs and increase customer satisfaction and retention.

4. Offering Value-Added Services: Provide exceptional customer service and offer value-added services to differentiate your business from competitors.

Consider implementing loyalty programs, discounts, and exclusive offers to incentivize repeat purchases and foster long-term relationships with customers.

5. Engaging with Customers: Actively engage with customers through various communication channels such as social media, email, and customer feedback platforms. Respond promptly to inquiries, address customer concerns, and solicit feedback to demonstrate your commitment to customer satisfaction and build trust.

6. Implementing Referral Programs: Encourage satisfied customers to refer your business to their network by offering incentives or rewards for successful referrals. Word-of-mouth marketing is a powerful tool for acquiring new customers and building credibility for your brand.

7. Monitoring and Analyzing Customer Acquisition Metrics: Track key performance indicators (KPIs) related to customer acquisition, such as conversion rates, cost per acquisition, and customer lifetime value. Analyze these metrics regularly to identify areas for improvement and optimize your customer acquisition strategies for maximum effectiveness.

8. Continuous Optimization and Testing: Continuously test and optimize your customer acquisition strategies to improve conversion rates and ROI. Experiment with different marketing tactics, messaging, and promotions to identify what resonates best with your target audience and adjust your approach accordingly.

By implementing these customer acquisition strategies effectively, you can attract new customers, enhance customer loyalty, and drive sustainable growth for your business. Remember that customer acquisition is an ongoing process that requires dedication, flexibility, and a customer-centric approach to succeed in today's competitive business landscape.

Advertising and Promotion

Advertising and promotion are crucial components of any business plan as they are essential for attracting customers, increasing brand visibility, and generating sales. In this section, we will delve into the various tactics and strategies that can be employed to effectively promote a business through multiple channels.

1. Digital Marketing:

In today's digital age, online advertising has become a cornerstone of marketing strategies. Businesses can utilize various digital marketing channels such as social media, search engine optimization (SEO), pay-per-click (PPC) advertising, email marketing, and content marketing to reach their target audience. Leveraging these channels allows businesses to engage with customers, drive website traffic, and increase brand awareness.

2. Social Media Marketing:

Social media platforms like Facebook, Instagram, Twitter, LinkedIn, and Pinterest offer powerful tools for businesses to connect with their audience. By creating engaging content, running targeted ads, and interacting with followers, businesses can build brand loyalty, drive engagement, and ultimately boost sales.

3. Search Engine Optimization (SEO):

Optimizing your website for search engines is essential for improving your online visibility and driving organic traffic. By using relevant keywords, creating quality content, and optimizing your website structure, you can improve your search engine rankings and attract more potential customers to your site.

4. Pay-Per-Click (PPC) Advertising:

PPC advertising allows businesses to place ads on search engines and websites and pay a fee each time their ad is clicked. This form of advertising is highly targeted and can yield quick results, making it an effective way to drive traffic and conversions.

5. Email Marketing:
Email marketing remains a powerful tool for businesses to nurture leads, communicate with customers, and promote products or services. By sending targeted and personalized emails, businesses can engage with their audience, drive sales, and build customer relationships.

6. Content Marketing:
Creating valuable and relevant content such as blog posts, videos, infographics, and whitepapers can help businesses establish authority in their industry and attract a loyal following. Content marketing is a long-term strategy that can drive organic traffic, increase brand awareness, and generate leads.

7. Traditional Advertising:
While digital marketing has gained prominence, traditional advertising methods such as print ads, radio spots, TV commercials, and direct mail still hold value. Depending on the target audience and budget, businesses can integrate traditional advertising into their promotional mix to reach a wider demographic.

8. Public Relations:
Building positive relationships with the media and influencers can help businesses generate buzz, increase credibility, and reach a larger audience. Press releases, media outreach, and partnerships with influencers can all contribute to a successful public relations strategy.

9. Events and Sponsorships:
Participating in industry events, hosting seminars or workshops, and sponsoring local community events are all effective ways to promote your business and

connect with potential customers face-to-face. These activities can help build brand awareness, foster relationships, and drive sales.

By incorporating a mix of digital marketing, traditional advertising, public relations, and events into your advertising and promotion strategy, businesses can create a comprehensive and effective plan to reach their target audience, drive engagement, and ultimately grow their business. It is important to continually evaluate and adjust your tactics based on performance metrics and market trends to ensure the success of your advertising and promotion efforts.

Chapter 7

Operations Plan

Operational Workflow

Operational workflow is a critical component of any business plan as it outlines the detailed processes and procedures that drive the day-to-day operations of a company. A well-defined operational workflow ensures that tasks are performed efficiently, resources are utilized effectively, and objectives are met in a timely manner. In this section, we will delve into the key aspects of operational workflow, including how to describe daily operations and processes effectively.

1. Defining Daily Operations: Daily operations encompass the routine activities that are essential for the functioning of the business. This includes tasks such as order processing, inventory management, customer service, production processes, and more. It is crucial to provide a comprehensive overview of each operational aspect, detailing the specific steps involved, responsibilities of staff members, and any technology or tools utilized to streamline operations.

2. Process Documentation: Documenting processes is crucial for ensuring consistency and efficiency in daily operations. This includes creating detailed Standard Operating Procedures (SOPs) for each key process, outlining step-by-step instructions, timelines, and quality standards. By clearly defining processes, employees can perform their tasks effectively, reducing errors and improving productivity.

3. Workflow Management: Managing workflow involves coordinating tasks, resources, and information flow to ensure smooth operations. This includes assigning responsibilities, setting priorities, and establishing communication channels to facilitate collaboration among team members. Effective workflow management helps in optimizing resource allocation, reducing bottlenecks, and improving overall operational performance.

4. Quality Control Measures: Implementing quality control measures is essential to maintain the standard of products or services delivered by the business. This includes establishing quality checkpoints, conducting regular inspections, and addressing any deviations from quality standards promptly. By incorporating quality control procedures into the operational workflow, businesses can enhance customer satisfaction and reputation.

5. Risk Management: Identifying and mitigating operational risks is crucial for business sustainability. This involves assessing potential risks that could impact daily operations, such as supply chain disruptions, technology failures, or regulatory compliance issues. Developing contingency plans and risk mitigation strategies within the operational workflow helps in minimizing disruptions and ensuring business continuity.

6. Continuous Improvement: Continuous evaluation and improvement of operational workflow are essential for adapting to changing market conditions and achieving operational excellence. This involves collecting feedback from employees, monitoring key performance indicators, and implementing process enhancements to optimize efficiency and effectiveness. By fostering a culture of continuous improvement, businesses can stay competitive and agile in a dynamic business environment.

In conclusion, a well-structured operational workflow is a cornerstone of a successful business plan, enabling businesses to achieve operational efficiency, maintain quality standards, and mitigate risks effectively. By clearly defining daily operations and processes, businesses can streamline their activities, enhance productivity, and ultimately drive sustainable growth. It is essential for businesses to regularly review and update their operational workflow to adapt to evolving business needs and market dynamics, ensuring long-term success and profitability.

Supply Chain Management

Supply chain management is a critical aspect of any business operation, as it involves the oversight and coordination of the flow of goods and services from suppliers to customers. Effective supply chain management ensures that products and services are delivered to the right place, at the right time, and in the right quantity. This section will delve into the key components of supply chain management, including managing suppliers, inventory, and logistics.

Managing Suppliers:

One of the key elements of supply chain management is establishing and maintaining relationships with suppliers. This involves identifying reliable suppliers, negotiating contracts, and monitoring performance to ensure quality and timely delivery of goods or services. It is essential for businesses to work closely with suppliers to build trust and collaboration, as well as to mitigate risks such as supply chain disruptions or quality issues. Regular communication and feedback mechanisms are crucial for fostering strong supplier relationships and addressing any issues that may arise.

Inventory Management:

Effective inventory management is essential for optimizing the balance between supply and demand. Businesses need to carefully monitor and control their inventory levels to avoid stockouts or excess inventory, which can lead to increased costs and operational inefficiencies. Inventory management involves forecasting demand, maintaining optimal stock levels, implementing efficient storage and tracking systems, and minimizing carrying costs. Utilizing inventory management software and tools can help businesses streamline their inventory processes and improve overall supply chain efficiency.

Logistics:

Logistics refers to the planning, coordination, and execution of the transportation and distribution of goods throughout the supply chain. This includes managing transportation routes, selecting carriers, tracking shipments, and ensuring timely delivery to customers. Effective logistics management requires careful planning, coordination, and optimization of resources to minimize transportation costs, reduce lead times, and enhance customer satisfaction. Businesses can leverage technology and data analytics to optimize their logistics operations, improve visibility and transparency, and identify opportunities for cost savings and process improvements.

Supply chain management plays a crucial role in enhancing overall operational efficiency, reducing costs, improving customer satisfaction, and gaining a competitive advantage in the marketplace. By effectively managing suppliers, inventory, and logistics, businesses can streamline their supply chain processes, minimize risks, and maximize value creation. It is important for businesses to continuously monitor and evaluate their supply chain performance, identify areas for improvement, and adapt to changing market dynamics to remain competitive and sustainable in the long run.

In conclusion, supply chain management is a multifaceted discipline that requires careful planning, coordination, and execution to ensure the seamless flow of goods and services throughout the supply chain. By focusing on managing suppliers, inventory, and logistics effectively, businesses can enhance their operational efficiency, optimize costs, and deliver value to customers. Embracing best practices in supply chain management can help businesses achieve a competitive edge and drive sustainable growth in today's dynamic business environment.

Technology and Equipment

In today's fast-paced business environment, technology and equipment play a crucial role in the operational efficiency and success of a business. In this section of the business plan, we will delve into the importance of identifying the necessary technology and equipment needed to support your business operations effectively.

1. Operational Workflow: Describing Daily Operations and Processes
To begin, it is essential to outline the operational workflow of your business. This involves detailing the day-to-day processes and activities that are essential for the smooth functioning of your business. Understanding your operational workflow will help you determine the specific technology and equipment required to streamline operations and enhance productivity.

2. Supply Chain Management: Managing Suppliers, Inventory, and Logistics
Efficient supply chain management is critical for ensuring timely delivery of products and services to customers. Identifying the technology and equipment needed to manage suppliers, track inventory levels, and optimize logistics processes is essential for maintaining a competitive edge in the market. This may include inventory management software, transportation management systems, and automated warehouse solutions.

3. Technology and Equipment: Identifying Necessary Tools and Resources
Next, it is important to identify the specific technology and equipment that will support your business operations. This may include hardware such as computers, servers, and networking devices, as well as software applications for accounting, customer relationship management (CRM), and project management. Additionally, specialized equipment related to your industry or production processes should be considered to ensure operational efficiency.

4. Staffing and Human Resources: Recruiting, Training, and Managing Employees

When considering technology and equipment needs, it is also essential to factor in the training and skills required for your workforce to effectively utilize these tools. Investing in employee training programs and providing ongoing support for using technology and equipment will help maximize their potential and contribute to overall business success.

5. Quality Control: Implementing Measures to Ensure Product/Service Quality

Lastly, technology and equipment play a critical role in maintaining quality control standards within your business. Implementing quality management systems, inspection tools, and testing equipment can help ensure that your products or services meet or exceed customer expectations. Monitoring and analyzing data through technology can also provide valuable insights for continuous improvement and innovation.

In conclusion, identifying the necessary technology and equipment for your business operations is a strategic decision that requires careful consideration and planning. By understanding your operational workflow, supply chain management needs, and quality control requirements, you can effectively determine the tools and resources that will support your business goals and objectives. Investing in the right technology and equipment will not only enhance operational efficiency but also position your business for long-term growth and success in today's competitive marketplace.

Staffing and Human Resources

Staffing and human resources are critical components of any business plan as they directly impact the success and sustainability of a company. Recruiting, training, and managing employees effectively can lead to increased productivity, employee satisfaction, and overall organizational performance. In this section, we will delve into the key aspects of staffing and human resources that should be considered when developing a business plan.

Recruiting: The process of recruiting the right talent for your business is crucial for achieving your company's goals. This involves identifying the skills and qualifications needed for each position, creating job descriptions, and implementing effective recruitment strategies. Whether you choose to recruit internally, use a recruiting agency, or leverage online job boards, it is essential to attract candidates who align with your company culture and values.

Training: Once you have hired new employees, investing in their training and development is essential for ensuring they can perform their roles effectively. Training programs should be designed to equip employees with the necessary skills and knowledge to excel in their positions. This may include on-the-job training, mentorship programs, workshops, and continued education opportunities. By investing in employee training, you can improve employee retention, job satisfaction, and overall performance.

Managing Employees: Effective management of employees involves creating a positive work environment, providing feedback and support, and promoting a culture of collaboration and teamwork. Managers play a crucial role in motivating and empowering their teams to achieve organizational goals. It is important to establish clear expectations, set performance goals, and provide regular feedback to help employees grow and succeed. Additionally, addressing any conflicts or performance issues in a timely and constructive manner is essential for maintaining a productive and harmonious work environment.

Legal Considerations: When developing your staffing and human resources plan, it is important to consider legal requirements related to employment, such as labor laws, workplace safety regulations, and discrimination laws. Ensuring compliance with these regulations will help protect your business from potential legal issues and liabilities. Additionally, having clear policies and procedures in place for hiring, training, and managing employees can help prevent misunderstandings and disputes in the workplace.

Employee Benefits and Compensation: Offering competitive benefits and compensation packages is key to attracting and retaining top talent. Consideration should be given to factors such as health insurance, retirement plans, paid time off, and other perks that can enhance employee satisfaction and loyalty. Additionally, developing a transparent and fair compensation structure based on market standards and employee performance can help motivate and retain your workforce.

Overall, staffing and human resources are integral components of a successful business plan. By prioritizing recruiting, training, and managing employees effectively, you can build a strong and resilient team that will drive your business forward. Investing in your employees not only benefits them individually but also contributes to the overall success and growth of your company.

Quality Control

Quality control is a crucial aspect of any business plan as it focuses on ensuring that products or services meet the expected standards of quality. Implementing effective quality control measures helps businesses maintain customer satisfaction, build a strong reputation, and drive success in the marketplace. In this section, we will delve into the key components of quality control and how to integrate them into your business plan.

1. Quality Standards and Specifications: The first step in quality control is to establish clear quality standards and specifications for your products or services. These standards should define the characteristics, features, and performance expectations that must be met to ensure customer satisfaction. By outlining these standards in your business plan, you demonstrate your commitment to delivering high-quality offerings to your target market.

2. Quality Assurance Processes: Quality assurance involves the systematic monitoring and evaluation of processes to ensure that quality standards are being met consistently. This includes implementing checkpoints, inspections, and testing procedures at various stages of production or service delivery. Describe in your business plan how you will integrate quality assurance processes into your operations to identify and address any deviations from the established standards.

3. Training and Skills Development: Quality control also relies on the skills and competencies of your workforce. Investing in training programs to enhance employee skills and knowledge about quality standards is essential. Your business plan should outline your approach to training and continuous skills development to ensure that all staff members are equipped to maintain quality standards in their respective roles.

4. Supplier Quality Management: If your business relies on suppliers for raw materials or components, it is essential to implement supplier quality management practices. This involves evaluating and selecting reliable suppliers, establishing quality requirements in supplier contracts, and conducting regular audits to ensure compliance with quality standards. Detail in your business plan how you will manage supplier quality to uphold the overall quality of your products or services.

5. Feedback and Improvement Processes: Quality control is an ongoing process that requires continuous feedback and improvement. Incorporate mechanisms for collecting customer feedback, monitoring product/service performance, and implementing corrective actions in response to quality issues. Demonstrate in your business plan your commitment to a culture of continuous improvement to enhance product/service quality over time.

6. Quality Metrics and Key Performance Indicators (KPIs): To measure the effectiveness of your quality control efforts, establish relevant quality metrics and KPIs to track performance against defined standards. Include in your business plan a section dedicated to outlining the key metrics you will use to assess quality levels and monitor progress towards quality improvement goals.

By addressing these aspects of quality control in your business plan, you showcase your dedication to delivering high-quality products or services that meet customer expectations and drive business success. Quality control is not just a one-time activity but a fundamental principle that should be integrated into your business operations to ensure long-term sustainability and competitiveness in the market.

Chapter 8

Financial Plan

Financial Statements

In the realm of business planning, financial statements play a crucial role in providing a comprehensive view of a company's financial health and performance. Understanding and effectively utilizing financial statements is essential for making informed decisions, attracting investors, and ensuring the long-term success of a business. In this section, we will delve into the key components of financial statements: income statements, balance sheets, and cash flow statements.

Income Statements:

An income statement, also known as a profit and loss statement, provides a snapshot of a company's financial performance over a specific period, typically a month, quarter, or year. It outlines the revenues generated by the business and subtracts the expenses incurred to calculate the net income or loss. The main components of an income statement include:

1. Revenue: This represents the total amount of money generated from sales of products or services.

2. Cost of Goods Sold (COGS): These are the direct costs associated with producing the goods or services sold by the company.

3. Gross Profit: Calculated by deducting COGS from revenue, gross profit reflects the profitability of the core business operations.

4. Operating Expenses: These are the costs incurred to run the business, such as salaries, rent, utilities, marketing, and administrative expenses.

5. Earnings Before Interest and Taxes (EBIT): Also known as operating income, EBIT is the profit generated before deducting interest and taxes.

6. Net Income: This is the final figure after subtracting all expenses, including interest and taxes, from the total revenue. Net income indicates the overall profitability of the business.

Balance Sheets:

A balance sheet provides a snapshot of a company's financial position at a specific point in time, typically the end of a financial period. It presents a detailed overview of the company's assets, liabilities, and shareholders' equity. The balance sheet follows the fundamental accounting equation: Assets = Liabilities + Shareholders' Equity. **The key components of a balance sheet include:**

1. Assets: These are resources owned by the company, such as cash, inventory, equipment, property, and accounts receivable.
2. Liabilities: These represent the company's obligations to creditors and suppliers, including loans, accounts payable, and accrued expenses.
3. Shareholders' Equity: **This reflects the owners' stake in the company and is** calculated as assets minus liabilities. It comprises common stock, retained earnings, and additional paid-in capital.

Cash Flow Statements:

A cash flow statement tracks the inflow and outflow of cash within a business over a specific period, providing insights into how cash is generated and utilized. It is divided into three main sections: operating activities, investing activities, and financing activities. The key components of a cash flow statement include:

1. Operating Activities: Cash flows from day-to-day business operations, including revenues, expenses, and working capital changes.
2. Investing Activities: Cash flows related to the purchase and sale of long-term assets, such as equipment, property, and investments.

3. Financing Activities: Cash flows from activities that affect the company's capital structure, such as issuing or repurchasing stock, taking out loans, or paying dividends.

In conclusion, financial statements are essential tools for evaluating a company's financial performance, stability, and growth potential. By understanding and analyzing income statements, balance sheets, and cash flow statements, business owners can make informed decisions, attract investors, and drive sustainable business growth. It is imperative for entrepreneurs to master the art of interpreting financial statements to navigate the complexities of business planning and financial management effectively.

Revenue Model

The revenue model is a crucial aspect of any business plan as it outlines how a company will generate income and sustain its operations. A well-defined revenue model not only helps in understanding the financial viability of the business but also provides insights into the scalability and growth potential. In this section, we will delve into the various components of a revenue model and discuss different strategies that businesses can adopt to earn money.

1. Revenue Streams: The first step in explaining the revenue model is to identify the primary sources of income for the business. This could include sales of products or services, subscription fees, licensing fees, advertising revenue, or any other form of monetization. It is important to clearly articulate how each revenue stream contributes to the overall financial health of the business.

2. Pricing Strategy: One of the key elements of the revenue model is the pricing strategy. Businesses need to determine the optimal pricing for their products or services based on factors such as cost of production, market demand, competition, and perceived value. Whether the business adopts a cost-plus pricing, value-based pricing, or penetration pricing strategy, it is essential to justify the chosen pricing approach in the business plan.

3. Revenue Projections: In this section, businesses should provide detailed forecasts of their revenue projections over a specific period, usually ranging from one to five years. These projections should be based on thorough market research, industry trends, and realistic assumptions. It is essential to include factors such as seasonality, market fluctuations, and growth potential in the revenue projections.

4. Sales Channels: Another critical component of the revenue model is the sales channels through which the business will reach its customers. This could include direct sales through a website, retail distribution, e-commerce platforms, partnerships with other businesses, or a combination of these channels. Businesses should outline the advantages and challenges associated with each sales channel and how they plan to optimize sales and revenue generation.

5. Customer Acquisition Strategy: To ensure a steady flow of revenue, businesses need to have a robust customer acquisition strategy in place. This could involve various marketing and sales tactics aimed at attracting and retaining customers. Businesses should outline their customer acquisition cost, customer lifetime value, and strategies for increasing customer loyalty and engagement.

6. Monetization of Additional Services: Apart from core products or services, businesses can explore additional revenue streams through complementary offerings or value-added services. This could include upselling, cross-selling, subscription-based services, or freemium models. Businesses should outline how these additional services will contribute to overall revenue generation and customer satisfaction.

7. Revenue Diversification: It is advisable for businesses to diversify their revenue streams to mitigate risks and capitalize on new opportunities. This could involve expanding into new markets, introducing new products or services, or exploring strategic partnerships. Businesses should assess the potential impact of revenue diversification on their overall financial stability and growth prospects.

In conclusion, the revenue model is a critical component of the business plan that outlines how a company will generate income and sustain its operations. By clearly defining revenue streams, pricing strategies, sales channels, customer acquisition tactics, and revenue projections, businesses can demonstrate their financial viability and growth potential to stakeholders. A well-thought-out revenue model not only serves as a roadmap for revenue generation but also helps in making informed decisions to optimize business performance and profitability.

Funding Requirements

One of the critical aspects of creating a comprehensive business plan is outlining the funding requirements for your venture. In this section, you will delve into the specifics of determining how much capital your business needs and how it will be utilized to support various aspects of your operations and growth strategies.

Determining the Capital Needs:

To start, you must conduct a thorough assessment of your financial requirements. This involves analyzing all the costs associated with launching and running your business. Consider factors such as startup costs, operational expenses, marketing and advertising budgets, staffing costs, technology investments, inventory purchases, and any other financial outlays essential for your business to function effectively.

It is essential to break down your funding needs into different categories to provide a clear picture of where the capital will be allocated. For instance, you may need funds for initial setup costs, ongoing operational expenses, marketing campaigns, research and development, and contingencies for unforeseen circumstances.

Utilization of Capital:

Once you have identified the total capital needed, you should detail how the funds will be utilized to drive the growth and success of your business. Create a comprehensive breakdown of the expenses and investments involved in various aspects of your operations:

1. Startup Costs: Outline the initial expenses required to launch your business, such as equipment purchases, lease deposits, legal fees, licenses, and permits.

2. Operational Expenses: Detail the ongoing costs necessary to sustain your business, including rent, utilities, salaries, insurance, maintenance, and other day-to-day expenditures.

3. Marketing and Advertising Budget: Specify the funds allocated for promoting your products or services, building brand awareness, and attracting customers through various marketing channels.

4. Research and Development: If applicable, explain the budget set aside for product innovation, market research, and enhancing your offerings to meet customer needs.

5. Staffing and Training: Describe the costs associated with hiring and training employees, as well as any benefits or incentives provided to ensure a skilled and motivated workforce.

6. Technology and Infrastructure: Identify the investments required for technology solutions, software, hardware, and infrastructure improvements to support your business operations effectively.

7. Contingency Fund: Include a buffer for unexpected expenses or emergencies to ensure your business can withstand unforeseen challenges without compromising its operations.

By providing a detailed breakdown of your funding requirements and how the capital will be utilized, you demonstrate a clear understanding of your financial needs and a strategic approach to managing resources effectively. Investors and lenders will appreciate the transparency and thoroughness of your financial planning, increasing their confidence in your business's potential for success. Remember to regularly review and update your funding requirements as your business grows and evolves to ensure ongoing financial stability and sustainability.

Financial Projections

Financial projections are a critical component of any business plan as they provide a roadmap for the financial health and viability of your business. By forecasting revenue, expenses, and profitability, you can effectively plan for the future, make informed decisions, and attract potential investors or lenders. In this section, we will delve into the key aspects of creating financial projections and how they contribute to the overall success of your business plan.

1. Overview of Financial Statements:

Financial projections typically include three main financial statements: income statement, balance sheet, and cash flow statement. These statements provide a comprehensive view of your business's financial performance, position, and cash flow. The income statement shows your revenue, expenses, and net income over a specific period. The balance sheet outlines your assets, liabilities, and equity at a specific point in time. The cash flow statement tracks the inflow and outflow of cash in your business.

2. Revenue Model:
Your revenue model outlines how your business will generate income. This could include details on pricing strategies, sales volume projections, and revenue streams. It is essential to clearly define your revenue sources and quantify your expected revenue based on market research, customer analysis, and sales projections.

3. Expense Projections:
Estimating your expenses accurately is crucial for determining your business's financial health. Expenses can include costs related to production, marketing, operations, salaries, rent, utilities, and more. By forecasting your expenses, you can plan for cost management, identify areas for optimization, and ensure that your business remains financially sustainable.

4. Funding Requirements:
In your financial projections, it is essential to outline your funding requirements to support your business operations and growth plans. This could include initial startup costs, working capital needs, equipment purchases, marketing expenses, and more. By clearly defining your funding needs, you can demonstrate to potential investors or lenders how their investment will be utilized and how it will contribute to your business's success.

5. Profitability Forecast:
Profitability forecasting involves projecting your business's potential profitability over a specific period. This includes estimating your gross profit margin, net profit margin, and break-even point. By analyzing your revenue and expenses, you can determine when your business is expected to become profitable and achieve financial sustainability. Profitability forecasting is crucial

for assessing the viability of your business model and making strategic decisions to improve profitability.

6. Sensitivity Analysis:
In addition to creating financial projections, conducting a sensitivity analysis can help you evaluate the impact of different variables on your financial performance. This involves testing various scenarios, such as changes in sales volume, pricing, or expenses, to understand how these factors may affect your business's profitability. By conducting a sensitivity analysis, you can prepare for potential risks, uncertainties, and market fluctuations that may impact your financial projections.

In conclusion, financial projections play a vital role in the business planning process by providing a detailed forecast of your business's financial performance. By creating accurate revenue, expense, and profitability projections, you can demonstrate the financial viability of your business, make informed strategic decisions, and attract potential investors or lenders. It is essential to regularly review and update your financial projections to reflect changes in the market, industry trends, and business operations, ensuring that your business plan remains dynamic and adaptable to evolving circumstances.

Break-Even Analysis
A Break-Even Analysis is a crucial component of a business plan that helps entrepreneurs determine the point at which their business will start to make a profit. By analyzing the relationship between costs, revenue, and profit, a Break-Even Analysis provides valuable insights into the financial health and sustainability of a business.

To calculate the break-even point, several key factors need to be considered:

1. Fixed Costs: Fixed costs are expenses that remain constant regardless of the volume of goods or services produced. These may include rent, salaries, utilities, insurance, and other overhead expenses.

2. Variable Costs: Variable costs are expenses that fluctuate based on the level of production or sales. These costs may include raw materials, labor, shipping, and marketing expenses.

3. Selling Price: The selling price is the amount at which a product or service is sold to customers. It is essential to determine the selling price accurately to ensure profitability.

4. Contribution Margin: The contribution margin is the difference between the selling price and variable costs per unit. It represents the amount of revenue available to cover fixed costs and contribute to profit.

The Break-Even Point can be calculated using the following formula:

Break-Even Point (in units) = Fixed Costs / (Selling Price per Unit - Variable Costs per Unit)

Once the Break-Even Point in units is determined, it can also be expressed in terms of sales revenue by multiplying the Break-Even Point in units by the selling price per unit.

Break-Even Point (in sales revenue) = Break-Even Point (in units) x Selling Price per Unit

Understanding the Break-Even Analysis is essential for businesses for several reasons:

1. Financial Planning: By knowing the Break-Even Point, businesses can set realistic sales goals and develop effective pricing strategies to ensure profitability.

2. Risk Management: The Break-Even Analysis helps businesses assess the impact of changes in costs, pricing, or sales volume on their financial performance.

3. Decision-Making: Businesses can use the Break-Even Analysis to evaluate the feasibility of new projects, product lines, or expansion plans.

4. Performance Evaluation: Monitoring actual sales against the Break-Even Point allows businesses to track their progress and make informed decisions to improve profitability.

It is important to note that the Break-Even Analysis is a dynamic tool that should be regularly reviewed and updated as business conditions change. By integrating the Break-Even Analysis into the financial planning process, businesses can enhance their strategic decision-making and improve their long-term financial sustainability.

In conclusion, the Break-Even Analysis is a valuable tool for entrepreneurs to assess the financial viability of their business ventures and make informed decisions to achieve profitability. By understanding the relationship between costs, revenue, and profit, businesses can optimize their operations and set a solid foundation for long-term success.

Chapter 9

Appendices and Supporting Documents

Supporting Documents

Supporting documents play a crucial role in a comprehensive business plan as they provide additional information and evidence to support the claims and projections made throughout the document. These documents help enhance the credibility and thoroughness of your business plan, giving readers a deeper insight into the operational and legal aspects of your business. In this chapter, we will delve into the various types of supporting documents that can be included in your business plan and why they are essential.

Resumes are one of the most common supporting documents included in a business plan, especially for startups or small businesses where the founding team plays a significant role in the success of the venture. Resumes provide detailed information about the qualifications, experience, and expertise of key team members, showcasing their capabilities and demonstrating why they are well-suited to lead the business to success. Investors and lenders often scrutinize the resumes of the management team to assess their competence and suitability for the roles they hold within the company.

Permits and licenses are crucial documents that demonstrate your compliance with regulatory requirements and legal obligations. Including copies of permits, licenses, and certifications relevant to your industry shows that your business operates within the confines of the law and adheres to industry standards. This instills confidence in stakeholders and mitigates risks associated with regulatory non-compliance, thus enhancing the overall credibility of your business plan.

Legal agreements are another vital component of supporting documents, especially when detailing partnerships, contracts, or agreements that are integral to the operation of your business. These agreements may include partnership agreements, supplier contracts, customer agreements, intellectual property licenses, or any other legal documents that are essential for the functioning of your business. By including these legal agreements in your business plan, you provide transparency and clarity regarding the legal framework within which your business operates.

Financial documents such as financial statements, tax returns, and bank statements offer an in-depth look into the financial health and performance of your business. These documents provide concrete evidence of your revenue, expenses, cash flow, and profitability, supporting the financial projections and assumptions outlined in your business plan. Investors and lenders rely on these financial documents to assess the financial viability and sustainability of your business, making them critical components of the overall business plan.

Other relevant documents that can be included as supporting materials in your business plan may vary depending on the nature of your business and industry. These could include market research reports, industry analyses, customer surveys, product prototypes, marketing collateral, and any other documents that provide additional context and validation for your business concept and strategies.

In conclusion, supporting documents serve as the backbone of a well-rounded business plan, offering validation, credibility, and transparency to your business concept and strategies. By including resumes, permits, legal agreements, financial documents, and other relevant materials, you bolster the strength of your business plan and increase the confidence of stakeholders in the potential success of your venture. Remember, the quality and relevance of supporting documents can make a significant difference in how your business plan is perceived and evaluated, so ensure that these documents are accurate, up-to-date, and effectively support the key points and projections outlined in your plan.

Additional Research

In the process of developing a comprehensive business plan, conducting thorough research is critical to understanding the market landscape and industry trends that will impact your business. Additional research involves gathering detailed market research and industry reports to support your business strategy and decision-making. This section delves into the importance of additional research, the types of data to collect, and how to effectively incorporate this information into your business plan.

Importance of Additional Research:

In today's dynamic business environment, staying informed about market trends, consumer behavior, competitive landscape, and industry forecasts is essential for making informed decisions and developing a successful business strategy. Additional research provides valuable insights that can help you identify opportunities, mitigate risks, and position your business competitively in the market.

Types of Data to Collect:

When conducting additional research for your business plan, consider gathering the following types of data:

1. Market Trends: Analyze current and emerging trends in your industry to anticipate shifts in consumer preferences, technological advancements, regulatory changes, and other factors that may impact your business.

2. Competitive Analysis: Study your competitors' strategies, strengths, weaknesses, and market positioning to identify opportunities for differentiation and competitive advantage.

3. Consumer Behavior: Understand your target market's needs, preferences, purchasing behavior, and demographics to tailor your products or services to meet their expectations effectively.

4. Industry Reports: Access industry-specific reports, market analyses, and economic forecasts to gain a deeper understanding of the overall market dynamics and growth potential in your industry.

5. Customer Surveys and Feedback: Collect customer feedback through surveys, focus groups, or interviews to gain insights into customer satisfaction, preferences, and pain points that can inform your marketing and product development strategies.

Incorporating Research Findings into Your Business Plan:

Once you have gathered relevant market research and industry reports, it's crucial to effectively incorporate these findings into your business plan. Here are some key steps to consider:

1. Summarize Key Insights: Provide a concise summary of the most critical findings from your research, highlighting key trends, opportunities, and threats that may impact your business.

2. Support Assumptions and Projections: Use data from market research to validate your assumptions and projections regarding market size, growth potential, target market demographics, and competitive landscape.

3. Identify Competitive Advantages: Showcase how your business leverages market insights to differentiate itself from competitors and capitalize on emerging opportunities in the market.

4. Mitigate Risks: Address potential risks and challenges identified through research and outline strategies to mitigate these risks effectively.

5. Update Regularly: Keep your market research up-to-date by monitoring industry trends, consumer behavior, and competitive developments to ensure your business plan remains relevant and aligned with market dynamics.

In conclusion, conducting additional research and incorporating detailed market research and industry reports into your business plan is essential for making informed strategic decisions, identifying growth opportunities, and ensuring the long-term success of your business. By leveraging data-driven insights, you can position your business competitively, anticipate market changes, and adapt your strategies to meet evolving customer needs and market demands.

Glossary of Terms

The Glossary of Terms section in a business plan serves as a comprehensive reference guide that defines and explains technical terms and jargon used throughout the document. This section is essential for ensuring clarity and understanding among readers who may not be familiar with specific industry terminology. By providing clear definitions and explanations, the Glossary of Terms helps to eliminate confusion and misinterpretation, enabling all stakeholders to grasp the concepts and information presented in the business plan effectively.

1. Market Research Terminology:
- **Primary Research:** Direct data collection from original sources.
- **Secondary Research:** Indirect data obtained from existing sources.

- **Demographics:** Statistical data relating to population characteristics.
- **Psychographics:** Analysis of consumer lifestyles, values, and attitudes.

2. Financial Terms:
- **Gross Profit:** Revenue minus the cost of goods sold.
- **Net Profit:** Total revenue minus all expenses.
- **ROI (Return on Investment):** Ratio of net profit to the initial investment.
- **Cash Flow:** Movement of money in and out of the business.

3. Marketing and Sales Vocabulary:
- **Target Market:** Specific group of consumers a business aims to reach.
- **Conversion Rate:** Percentage of leads that result in sales.
- **Brand Equity:** Value associated with a brand's reputation and recognition.
- **SWOT Analysis:** Examination of a business's Strengths, Weaknesses, Opportunities, and Threats.

4. Legal and Compliance Terms:
- **Intellectual Property:** Intangible assets like patents, trademarks, and copyrights.
- **Trademark:** Symbol, word, or design that distinguishes a brand.
- **Compliance:** Adherence to laws, regulations, and industry standards.

5. Operational Definitions:
- **Supply Chain:** Network of suppliers and processes delivering products/services.
- **Quality Control:** Procedures to ensure products/services meet standards.
- **Workflow:** Sequence of tasks in a business process.

6. Strategic Planning Concepts:
- **Mission Statement:** Purpose and values guiding a company's actions.
- **Vision Statement:** Aspirational description of a company's future state.

- **Competitive Advantage:** Unique factors that set a business apart from rivals.

7. Financial Statements Terminology:
- **Income Statement:** Report showing revenues, expenses, and profits over a period.
- **Balance Sheet:** Snapshot of a company's assets, liabilities, and equity.
- **Cash Flow Statement:** Summary of cash inflows and outflows.

Including a Glossary of Terms in the business plan not only enhances clarity and comprehension but also demonstrates the author's professionalism and attention to detail. It ensures that readers, whether investors, partners, or internal stakeholders, can easily navigate the document and grasp the intricate concepts presented. By defining technical terms and industry-specific jargon, the Glossary of Terms adds value to the overall business plan and contributes to its effectiveness in communicating the business's strategy and objectives.

Charts and Graphs

Charts and Graphs are essential components of a business plan as they provide visual aids to support the data and projections presented in the document. They help to convey complex information in a clear and concise manner, making it easier for readers to understand key insights and trends. In this section, we will discuss the importance of including Charts and Graphs in your business plan, the types of visual aids you can use, and best practices for incorporating them effectively.

Importance of Charts and Graphs in a Business Plan:

1. Enhanced Data Visualization: Charts and Graphs help in presenting data in a visually appealing format, making it easier for readers to interpret and analyze the information.

2. Clarity and Conciseness: Visual aids can simplify complex data sets and trends, allowing stakeholders to grasp key points quickly without getting lost in numbers and text.

3. Impactful Communication: Visual representations can make a stronger impact than text alone, helping to strengthen your argument and showcase the potential of your business.

4. Supporting Projections: Charts and Graphs can lend credibility to your financial forecasts, market trends, and growth projections by presenting them in a visual format.

Types of Visual Aids to Include in Your Business Plan:

1. Line Graphs: Ideal for showing trends over time, such as revenue growth, market share, or customer acquisition.

2. Bar Graphs: Useful for comparing different categories or variables, such as sales by product category or market share by region.

3. Pie Charts: Effective for illustrating proportions and percentages, such as market segmentation or revenue distribution.

4. Tables: Helpful for presenting detailed numerical data, such as financial statements or market research findings.

5. Infographics: Creative visual representations that combine text, images, and charts to convey complex information in a visually engaging way.

Best Practices for Incorporating Charts and Graphs:

1. Relevance: Ensure that the visual aids you include directly support the data and analysis presented in the corresponding sections of your business plan.

2. Clarity: Use clear and easy-to-understand formats, labels, and legends to help readers interpret the information accurately.

3. Consistency: Maintain a consistent style and color scheme throughout your visual aids to create a cohesive and professional look.

4. Balance: Avoid overwhelming your audience with an excessive number of charts and graphs; focus on including only the most relevant and impactful visuals.

5. Interpretation: Provide brief explanations or captions for each chart or graph to guide readers on how to interpret the data presented.

6. Accessibility: Ensure that your visual aids are accessible to all readers, including those with visual impairments, by providing alternative text or descriptions where necessary.

In conclusion, incorporating Charts and Graphs in your business plan can significantly enhance the clarity, credibility, and impact of your presentation. By choosing the right types of visual aids, following best practices for their inclusion, and ensuring their relevance and accuracy, you can effectively communicate your business's potential and make a compelling case to investors, lenders, and stakeholders.

References

References play a crucial role in a business plan as they provide credibility and support for the information presented. Citing sources and references used in your research and planning not only enhances the validity of your business plan but also demonstrates a thorough and well-informed approach to your strategic initiatives. Here is a detailed discussion on how to effectively include references in your business plan:

1. Importance of References:

Including a references section in your business plan is essential for several reasons. Firstly, it shows that your plan is based on reliable and accurate information obtained from credible sources. This can help instill confidence in potential investors, lenders, or stakeholders who may review your plan. Secondly, it allows readers to verify the data and research you have conducted, ensuring transparency and authenticity in your business proposal.

2. Types of Sources to Reference:

When citing sources in your business plan, it is important to include a variety of reputable sources to support your claims and analysis. These may include industry reports, market research studies, academic journals, government publications, financial data from recognized sources, and expert opinions from professionals in the field. By referencing a diverse range of sources, you can strengthen the credibility of your plan and provide a well-rounded perspective on the market and industry landscape.

3. Formatting References:

The references section in your business plan should follow a consistent and recognized citation style, such as APA, MLA, or Chicago. Each reference entry should include key details such as the author's name, publication title, publication date, and source URL if applicable. Organize your references alphabetically by author's last name or by publication title to ensure clarity and ease of reference for readers. Additionally, be sure to provide full and accurate citations for all sources used in your plan to avoid plagiarism and uphold academic integrity.

4. In-Text Citations:

hroughout your business plan, it is important to include in-text citations whenever you refer to or paraphrase information from external sources. This helps attribute credit to the original authors and avoids any accusations of plagiarism. In-text citations should be brief and provide enough information for readers to locate the full reference in the references section. Consistency in citation style and format is key to maintaining professionalism and academic rigor in your plan.

5. Acknowledging Sources:

In addition to citing sources within the main body of your business plan, it is also important to acknowledge and thank any individuals or organizations that provided valuable insights or data during the research process. This can be done in a separate acknowledgments section or within the executive summary to show appreciation for their contributions and support.

6. Reviewing and Updating References:

As you finalize your business plan, make sure to thoroughly review and double-check all references for accuracy and completeness. Update any outdated sources or broken links to ensure that your plan is based on the most current and relevant information available. Regularly revisiting and updating your references can help maintain the credibility and relevance of your business plan over time.

In conclusion, referencing sources in your business plan is a fundamental aspect of creating a well-informed and persuasive document. By citing reputable sources, following established citation guidelines, and acknowledging contributions from others, you can enhance the credibility and professionalism of your plan, ultimately increasing its impact and effectiveness in attracting support for your business endeavors.

Chapter 10

Review and Presentation

Reviewing Your Business Plan

Once you have completed drafting your business plan, it is essential to review and revise it thoroughly to ensure its effectiveness and accuracy. Reviewing your business plan is a critical step in the process as it allows you to fine-tune your strategy, identify potential gaps or inconsistencies, and make necessary adjustments before presenting it to stakeholders. In this section, we will discuss various techniques for self-review and revision to help you create a comprehensive and compelling business plan.

1. Start with a Structured Approach: Begin by reviewing your business plan in a systematic manner. Break down the document into sections and focus on one section at a time. This approach will help you to concentrate on specific aspects of your plan and ensure that each area is thoroughly examined for clarity and coherence.

2. Check for Consistency and Coherence: Verify that all sections of your business plan are consistent with each other and align cohesively to present a unified strategy. Ensure that your objectives, market analysis, and financial projections are in harmony and support the overall vision and goals of your business.

3. Assess Clarity and Readability: Review the language and tone of your business plan to ensure that it is clear, concise, and easily understandable. Avoid jargon or technical terms that may confuse readers and strive for a professional and engaging writing style that captures the essence of your business effectively.

4. Validate Data and Assumptions: Double-check all data, statistics, and assumptions presented in your business plan to ensure their accuracy and relevance. Verify that your market research, financial projections, and competitive analysis are based on reliable sources and sound reasoning to enhance the credibility of your plan.

5. Seek Feedback from Others: Consider sharing your business plan with trusted advisors, mentors, or peers to gather valuable feedback and perspectives. Their insights can provide fresh viewpoints and identify potential blind spots or areas for improvement that you may have overlooked during the drafting process.

6. Conduct a SWOT Analysis: Apply the SWOT (Strengths, Weaknesses, Opportunities, Threats) framework to evaluate your business plan objectively. Identify the key strengths and weaknesses of your strategy, opportunities for growth, and potential threats or challenges that may impact your business's success.

7. Review Financial Projections: Scrutinize your financial projections carefully to ensure they are realistic, achievable, and aligned with your business objectives. Verify that your revenue forecasts, expenses, and cash flow projections are based on sound assumptions and reflect a sustainable financial plan.

8. Update for Relevance: Keep your business plan current and relevant by incorporating any new developments, market trends, or changes in your business environment. Regularly update your plan to reflect the evolving needs and goals of your business and ensure it remains a dynamic and strategic roadmap for success.

9. Conduct a Final Proofreading: Before finalizing your business plan, conduct a final proofreading to check for any spelling or grammatical errors, formatting inconsistencies, or typographical mistakes. A well-presented and error-free document conveys professionalism and attention to detail to your audience.

In conclusion, reviewing your business plan is a crucial step in the business planning process that requires diligence, attention to detail, and a critical eye for improvement. By following these techniques for self-review and revision, you can enhance the quality and effectiveness of your business plan, increase its impact on stakeholders, and position your business for success in the competitive marketplace.

Getting Feedback

Seeking feedback on your business plan is a crucial step in the planning process. Input from mentors, advisors, and peers can provide valuable insights, identify blind spots, and help you refine your strategy for success. Here is a detailed explanation of how to effectively seek feedback from these key sources:

1. Mentors:

Mentors are experienced individuals who can provide guidance, advice, and support based on their own success in the business world. When seeking feedback from mentors, consider the following tips:

- Choose mentors who have relevant expertise in your industry or business niche.
- Clearly communicate your goals and objectives to help them provide targeted feedback.
- Be open to constructive criticism and be willing to implement suggested changes.
- Schedule regular check-ins with your mentors to track your progress and receive ongoing guidance.

2. Advisors:

Advisors are professionals with specialized knowledge in specific areas such as finance, marketing, or operations. When approaching advisors for feedback, consider the following best practices:

- Identify advisors who can offer insights in areas where you may lack expertise.
- Provide them with a clear overview of your business plan and specific areas where you seek feedback.
- Listen actively to their suggestions and ask clarifying questions to fully understand their perspective.
- Consider forming an advisory board with diverse expertise to gather comprehensive feedback from multiple sources.

3. Peers:

Peers are individuals in your network who may be at a similar stage in their entrepreneurial journey or have complementary skills and perspectives. When seeking feedback from peers, keep the following in mind:

- Choose peers who can provide honest and objective feedback without bias.
- Create a peer review group where members can exchange feedback on each other's business plans.
- Offer to review their plans in return to foster a mutually beneficial relationship.
- Consider organizing brainstorming sessions or workshops where peers can provide collective feedback and generate new ideas.

Overall, the key to effectively seeking feedback from mentors, advisors, and peers is to approach the process with an open mind, a willingness to listen, and a desire to continuously improve your business plan. Remember that feedback is a valuable tool for refining your strategy, identifying potential pitfalls, and maximizing your chances of success in the competitive business landscape. By incorporating feedback from these key sources, you can strengthen your business plan, enhance your decision-making process, and ultimately increase your chances of achieving your goals and objectives.

Finalizing the Document

Finalizing the document of your business plan is a critical step in the process that ensures the document is polished, professional, and ready to be presented to potential investors, lenders, or stakeholders. This stage requires attention to detail, thoroughness, and a keen eye for quality to make a lasting impression and instill confidence in the readers. Here are key considerations and best practices to follow when finalizing your business plan:

1. Proofreading and Editing: Before finalizing your business plan, it is essential to thoroughly proofread and edit the entire document. Check for spelling and grammar errors, consistency in formatting, and clarity in language. A well-edited document demonstrates professionalism and attention to detail.

2. Consistency and Cohesion: Ensure that the content flows logically and cohesively throughout the business plan. Each section should seamlessly connect to the next, guiding the reader through a clear and structured narrative. Consistent formatting, fonts, and styling enhance the overall readability and professionalism of the document.

3. Accuracy and Completeness: Verify that all the information presented in the business plan is accurate, up-to-date, and supported by data and research. Check financial projections, market analysis, and any other quantitative or qualitative data to ensure its validity. Completeness is key - make sure all sections are filled in and no critical details are missing.

4. Visual Appeal: Incorporate visuals such as charts, graphs, and images where relevant to enhance the visual appeal of your business plan. Visual aids can help communicate complex information more effectively and break up large blocks of text, making the document more engaging and easier to digest.

5. Professional Design: Pay attention to the design and layout of your business plan. Use a clean and professional template that aligns with your brand identity. Ensure that the font size and style are consistent, headings are clearly defined, and white space is appropriately utilized to improve readability.

6. Executive Summary Refinement: The executive summary is often the first section that readers will see, so it should be concise, compelling, and enticing. Refine the executive summary to capture the essence of your business plan succinctly, highlighting key points that will grab the reader's attention and pique their interest.

7. Peer Review and Feedback: Seek feedback from mentors, advisors, or peers who can provide valuable insights and suggestions for improvement. A fresh set of eyes can catch errors or inconsistencies that you may have overlooked and offer constructive feedback to enhance the overall quality of the plan.

8. Legal and Compliance Check: Ensure that your business plan adheres to legal and regulatory requirements. Verify that all necessary licenses, permits, and agreements are in place and that your business operations are compliant with relevant laws and regulations.

9. Executive Presentation: Consider how you will present your business plan to your target audience. Prepare for potential questions or areas of interest that may arise during the presentation. Practice delivering a compelling pitch that effectively conveys the value proposition and potential of your business.

10. Final Review and Approval: Once you have completed all the necessary revisions and refinements, conduct a final review of the entire document to ensure that it meets your standards of professionalism and completeness. Obtain any final approvals from key stakeholders before proceeding with presentations or submissions.

By following these guidelines and best practices, you can ensure that your business plan is finalized to a high standard of professionalism, completeness, and effectiveness. A well-crafted and polished document not only reflects positively on your business but also increases the likelihood of achieving your desired outcomes when presenting your plan to potential investors or partners.

Presenting Your Business Plan

Presenting your business plan to potential investors, lenders, or stakeholders is a critical step in securing the support and resources you need for your venture. A well-prepared and compelling presentation can make all the difference in convincing your audience of the viability and potential success of your business. Here are some key tips to keep in mind when pitching your business plan:

1. Know Your Audience:

Before you begin your presentation, it is crucial to understand who you are pitching to. Tailor your message and focus on aspects of your business plan that are most relevant to your audience. Investors may be interested in financial projections and potential returns, while lenders may be more concerned with your ability to repay a loan. Stakeholders may be looking for alignment with their values and goals.

2. Start with a Strong Introduction:

Capture your audience's attention from the start with a compelling introduction that clearly articulates your business concept, mission, and vision. Clearly communicate the problem your business solves and why your solution is unique and valuable. Make sure to highlight the key benefits and opportunities your business offers.

3. Focus on the Essentials:

During your presentation, focus on the most critical aspects of your business plan. Highlight key points such as market opportunity, competitive advantage, revenue model, and financial projections. Keep your presentation concise and to the point, emphasizing the most important information that will help your audience understand the potential of your business.

4. Use Visual Aids:

Visual aids such as charts, graphs, and images can help illustrate your key points and make complex information easier to understand. Use visuals to enhance your presentation and provide a clear and engaging way to communicate your data and projections.

5. Practice and Rehearse:

Practice your presentation multiple times to ensure that you are confident and well-prepared. Rehearse in front of a mirror or with a trusted friend or mentor to receive feedback and refine your delivery. Pay attention to your tone, body language, and pacing to ensure that you come across as professional and persuasive.

6. Anticipate Questions:

Be prepared to answer questions that may arise during your presentation. Anticipate potential concerns or areas of confusion and have thoughtful responses ready. Demonstrating your knowledge and preparedness will instill confidence in your audience and show that you have thoroughly considered all aspects of your business plan.

7. Be Open to Feedback:

Welcome feedback from your audience and be open to suggestions for improvement. Engage in a constructive dialogue with investors, lenders, or stakeholders to address any concerns and demonstrate your willingness to adapt and refine your plan based on feedback.

8. Close with a Strong Conclusion:

Conclude your presentation with a clear summary of key points and a call to action. Reinforce the value proposition of your business and emphasize why your venture is worth investing in. Leave your audience with a lasting impression and a sense of excitement about the potential of your business.

In conclusion, presenting your business plan effectively is essential for attracting the support and resources needed to bring your vision to life. By following these tips and approaching your presentation with confidence and professionalism, you can increase your chances of success and make a compelling case for why your business deserves investment or partnership.

Updating Your Plan

A business plan is not a static document but a dynamic roadmap that should evolve alongside your business. As your company grows and market conditions change, it is crucial to regularly update and revise your business plan to ensure its relevance and effectiveness. This section will explore the importance of updating your plan, key considerations for maintenance and revision, and best practices for keeping your business plan current.

Importance of Updating Your Plan:

As your business progresses, you may encounter new opportunities, challenges, and market trends that can impact your strategic direction. By updating your business plan regularly, you can adapt to these changes, seize emerging opportunities, and address potential risks proactively. Updating your plan also demonstrates your commitment to strategic planning and continuous improvement, which can enhance your credibility with stakeholders such as investors, lenders, and partners.

Key Considerations for Maintenance and Revision:

1. Regular Review: Schedule periodic reviews of your business plan to assess its alignment with your current goals, market conditions, and financial performance. Aim to review and update your plan at least annually, or more frequently if significant changes occur in your business environment.

2. Feedback and Input: Seek feedback from key stakeholders such as advisors, mentors, employees, and customers to gain diverse perspectives on your business strategy. Incorporating feedback can help you identify blind spots, refine your approach, and enhance the quality of your business plan.

3. Tracking Progress: Monitor key performance indicators (KPIs) and milestones outlined in your business plan to track your progress towards achieving your goals. Regularly evaluating your performance against your projections can help you identify deviations, adjust your strategies, and make informed decisions to drive business growth.

4. Scenario Planning: Anticipate potential market shifts, competitive threats, and internal challenges by conducting scenario planning exercises. Developing contingency plans and alternative strategies can help you mitigate risks and ensure your business remains resilient in a dynamic environment.

Best Practices for Keeping Your Business Plan Current:

1. Update Market Research: Stay informed about industry trends, customer preferences, and competitive landscape through ongoing market research. Incorporate new insights and data into your business plan to refine your market strategy and capitalize on emerging opportunities.

2. Revise Financial Projections: Adjust your financial projections based on actual performance, changing market conditions, and revised business assumptions. Regularly review your revenue forecasts, expense projections, and cash flow estimates to ensure they reflect your current financial outlook accurately.

3. Align Goals and Strategies: Evaluate the alignment between your business goals and operational strategies to ensure coherence and consistency in your approach. Update your objectives, action plans, and key initiatives to reflect your evolving priorities and strategic direction.

4. Communicate Changes: Keep your team, investors, and other stakeholders informed about updates to your business plan and the rationale behind the changes. Transparent communication can foster trust, collaboration, and support for your revised strategies, enhancing stakeholder engagement and buy-in.

In conclusion, updating your business plan is a continuous process that involves monitoring, evaluating, and adjusting your strategies to adapt to changing circumstances and drive sustainable growth. By staying proactive and agile in revising your plan, you can position your business for success, navigate challenges effectively, and seize new opportunities in a dynamic marketplace. Embrace the mindset of ongoing planning and strategic thinking to ensure your business remains competitive, resilient, and future-ready.

Conclusion

Summary of key points

The summary of key points in the book "How to Write a Business Plan" serves as a crucial wrap-up of the essential aspects covered throughout the guide. This section aims to consolidate the main takeaways and insights provided in the preceding chapters, offering a comprehensive overview for readers to reference and reflect upon. Let's delve into the key points highlighted in this summary:

1. The Importance of a Business Plan: The summary reiterates the significance of having a well-structured and comprehensive business plan. It emphasizes how a business plan serves as a roadmap for entrepreneurs, guiding them through the various stages of business development and helping them achieve their goals.

2. Understanding the Purpose of a Business Plan: The summary reinforces the core purpose of a business plan, which is to define the business, outline its objectives, and provide a strategic direction for future growth. It emphasizes the importance of tailoring the plan to different audiences, whether they are investors, lenders, or internal stakeholders.

3. Research and Analysis: The summary underscores the critical role of research and analysis in developing a solid business plan. It highlights the key components of market research, industry analysis, customer analysis, SWOT analysis, and competitive analysis, emphasizing how these insights inform strategic decision-making.

4. Executive Summary and Company Description: The summary emphasizes the significance of crafting a compelling executive summary that encapsulates the business concept, objectives, market opportunity, and financial highlights. It also stresses the importance of defining the company's structure, mission, vision, business model, and legal considerations.

5. Products or Services and Market Strategy: The summary highlights the importance of clearly defining the products or services offered, identifying the unique selling proposition, and outlining the pricing strategy and intellectual property considerations. It also emphasizes the need for a robust marketing plan, branding strategy, sales strategy, customer acquisition tactics, and advertising and promotion efforts.

6. Operations and Financial Planning: The summary underscores the importance of operational efficiency, supply chain management, technology utilization, staffing, and quality control in ensuring smooth business operations. It also emphasizes the significance of developing sound financial statements, revenue models, funding requirements, financial projections, and break-even analysis to sustain financial health and growth.

7. Review and Presentation: The summary provides guidance on reviewing and refining the business plan, seeking feedback from mentors and advisors, finalizing the document with professionalism, and presenting it effectively to investors and stakeholders. It also stresses the importance of updating the plan regularly to align with the evolving needs of the business.

8. Conclusion and Next Steps: The summary concludes by encouraging readers to take action and implement the business plan effectively. It offers final tips for ongoing planning and strategic thinking, motivating entrepreneurs to stay proactive and adaptive in their business endeavors.

In essence, the summary of key points serves as a comprehensive recapitulation of the critical elements covered in the book, empowering readers to distill the core insights and apply them in their business planning endeavors. It encapsulates the essence of strategic business planning and provides a roadmap for success in the competitive business landscape.

Encouragement to Take Action and Implement Your Business Plan

After diligently crafting a comprehensive business plan following the structured guidelines outlined in this book, it is crucial to emphasize the significance of taking proactive steps to implement the strategies and goals outlined in the document. While creating a well-thought-out business plan is an essential first step towards success, its true value lies in the execution and application of the proposed strategies. Here are some key points to consider when it comes to taking action and implementing your business plan:

1. Set Clear Objectives and Milestones: The business plan serves as a roadmap for your venture, outlining your short-term and long-term goals. It is essential to set clear objectives and establish measurable milestones to track your progress. By breaking down your goals into achievable targets, you can monitor your performance and make necessary adjustments along the way.

2. Allocate Resources Appropriately: Implementing your business plan requires allocating resources effectively, including financial, human, and technological resources. Ensure that you have the necessary resources in place to support the execution of your strategies. This might involve hiring skilled personnel, investing in technology, or securing funding as outlined in your financial plan.

3. Develop an Action Plan: Translate the strategies outlined in your business plan into actionable steps by creating a detailed action plan. Assign responsibilities, set deadlines, and establish accountability mechanisms to ensure that tasks are completed in a timely manner. Regularly review and update your action plan to stay on track and adapt to changing circumstances.

4. Monitor Progress and Evaluate Performance: Regularly monitor your progress against the goals and milestones set in your business plan. Track key performance indicators (KPIs) to gauge the effectiveness of your strategies and make informed decisions based on data-driven insights. Identify areas of success and areas that may require adjustments to optimize your business operations.

5. Adapt and Pivot When Necessary: The business landscape is dynamic, and unexpected challenges or opportunities may arise along the way. Be prepared to adapt and pivot your strategies as needed to stay competitive and responsive to market changes. Flexibility and agility are key traits of successful businesses that can navigate uncertainties and capitalize on emerging trends.

6. Seek Continuous Improvement: Implementing your business plan is an ongoing process that requires a commitment to continuous improvement. Encourage a culture of innovation and learning within your organization, where feedback is valued, and lessons learned are incorporated into future planning cycles. Embrace change as an opportunity for growth and evolution.

7. Celebrate Achievements and Stay Motivated: As you make progress towards achieving your business goals, take the time to celebrate milestones and acknowledge the hard work and dedication of your team. Recognizing achievements boosts morale and reinforces a sense of accomplishment, motivating you to stay focused and committed to realizing your vision.

In conclusion, while creating a business plan is a critical step in shaping the direction of your venture, the true test lies in the implementation of the strategies and tactics outlined in the document. By taking proactive steps, allocating resources effectively, monitoring progress, adapting to changes, and fostering a culture of continuous improvement, you can maximize the potential for success and achieve your business objectives. Remember that a well-executed business plan can serve as a powerful tool to guide your actions and drive your business towards sustainable growth and prosperity.

Final Tips for Ongoing Planning and Strategic Thinking

As you embark on the journey of creating and implementing your business plan, it is essential to understand that the process of planning is not a one-time event but rather a dynamic and ongoing practice. Here are some final tips to help you maintain the relevance and effectiveness of your business plan through ongoing planning and strategic thinking:

1. Embrace Flexibility: In today's rapidly changing business environment, it is crucial to remain flexible and adaptable. Your business plan should not be set in stone but rather serve as a guiding framework that can be adjusted and revised as needed. Be open to new opportunities, market trends, and feedback from stakeholders, and be willing to pivot your strategies when necessary.

2. Monitor Key Performance Indicators (KPIs): Establishing and tracking key performance indicators is essential for measuring the success of your business plan. Identify specific metrics that align with your business objectives and regularly monitor and analyze them to gauge your progress. This data-driven approach will help you make informed decisions and identify areas for improvement.

3. Conduct Regular Reviews and Updates: Set aside dedicated time intervals to review and update your business plan. It is recommended to conduct quarterly or bi-annual reviews to assess the performance of your business, analyze market trends, and make necessary adjustments to your strategies. By staying proactive and responsive, you can ensure that your business plan remains relevant and effective.

4. Foster a Culture of Innovation: Encourage a culture of innovation within your organization to stimulate creativity, generate new ideas, and drive continuous improvement. Embrace experimentation, encourage feedback from employees and customers, and be open to exploring innovative solutions that can propel your business forward. By fostering a culture of innovation, you can stay ahead of the competition and adapt to changing market dynamics.

5. Stay Informed and Educated: In the fast-paced business landscape, staying informed about industry trends, emerging technologies, and best practices is crucial for maintaining a competitive edge. Make a commitment to continuous learning by attending industry conferences, networking with peers, and seeking out educational resources to expand your knowledge and skills. By staying informed and educated, you can make well-informed decisions and drive innovation within your organization.

6. Cultivate Strategic Partnerships: Building strategic partnerships with other businesses, suppliers, or industry experts can provide valuable insights, resources, and opportunities for collaboration. Look for opportunities to leverage the expertise and resources of partners to enhance your business capabilities, expand your market reach, and drive mutual growth. Strategic partnerships can also help you stay agile and responsive to market changes by tapping into external knowledge and networks.

7. Seek Feedback and Advice: Don't hesitate to seek feedback and advice from mentors, advisors, and peers throughout the implementation of your business plan. Their external perspective and insights can offer valuable guidance, challenge your assumptions, and help you identify blind spots or areas for improvement. By soliciting feedback from trusted sources, you can gain valuable insights and refine your strategies for greater success.

In conclusion, ongoing planning and strategic thinking are essential for the long-term success and sustainability of your business. By embracing flexibility, monitoring KPIs, conducting regular reviews, fostering innovation, staying informed, cultivating partnerships, and seeking feedback, you can ensure that your business plan remains relevant, adaptive, and effective in navigating the ever-evolving business landscape. Remember that strategic planning is a continuous process that requires dedication, foresight, and agility to drive growth and achieve your business goals.

Appendices

Templates and Samples

Templates and samples are valuable resources that can greatly assist in the process of creating a comprehensive and well-structured business plan. These tools provide a framework and examples for each section of the plan, offering guidance on formatting, content, and overall presentation. In this section, we will delve into the importance of using templates and samples, discuss how they can benefit entrepreneurs, and provide insights on how to effectively leverage these resources.

One of the primary benefits of using templates and samples is that they offer a starting point for entrepreneurs who may be new to the business planning process. These resources provide a structured outline that can help organize thoughts, ideas, and information in a logical and cohesive manner. By following a template, individuals can ensure that they cover all essential components of a business plan, from the executive summary to financial projections, without overlooking critical details.

Moreover, templates and samples can serve as reference points for best practices in business planning. They showcase industry standards and conventions for each section of the plan, offering insights into what information is typically included and how it is presented. By studying samples, entrepreneurs can gain a better understanding of how to effectively communicate their business concept, market analysis, financial projections, and other key aspects of the plan to potential investors or stakeholders.

Templates and samples also help streamline the business planning process by saving time and effort. Instead of starting from scratch and struggling to structure a plan from the ground up, individuals can leverage existing templates to expedite the process. By customizing a template to fit their specific business needs and goals, entrepreneurs can focus on refining their strategy and fine-tuning their plan rather than getting bogged down in formatting and organization.

In addition, templates and samples can inspire creativity and innovation by providing examples of successful business plans that have effectively communicated a compelling vision and strategy. Entrepreneurs can draw inspiration from these examples, adapt proven strategies to their own business model, and tailor their plan to stand out in a competitive market. By studying different samples, individuals can learn from the strengths and weaknesses of others' plans and apply those insights to strengthen their own.

When utilizing templates and samples, it is important to customize them to reflect the unique aspects of your business. While templates offer a structured framework, it is essential to personalize the content to accurately represent your company's mission, vision, and goals. Tailoring the language, data, and strategies to align with your specific industry, target market, and competitive landscape will enhance the credibility and relevance of your business plan.

Furthermore, entrepreneurs should use templates and samples as guidelines rather than rigid rules. Flexibility is key in adapting the template to suit the evolving needs of your business and the preferences of your audience. By incorporating your own voice, insights, and creativity into the plan, you can create a document that authentically represents your vision and resonates with stakeholders.

In conclusion, templates and samples are invaluable tools that can simplify the business planning process, provide guidance on structure and content, and inspire innovation in crafting a compelling strategy. By leveraging these resources effectively, entrepreneurs can create a well-crafted business plan that communicates their vision, attracts potential investors, and sets a solid foundation for future growth and success.

Resources for Business Planning

When it comes to creating a comprehensive and effective business plan, leveraging the right resources can make all the difference. Whether you are a seasoned entrepreneur or a first-time business owner, having access to a variety of books, tools, and websites can provide valuable insights, guidance, and support throughout the planning process. Here are some recommended resources to help you craft a winning business strategy:

Books:

1. "Business Model Generation" by Alexander Osterwalder and Yves Pigneur: This book introduces the concept of the Business Model Canvas, a strategic tool for developing new or documenting existing business models.

2. "The Lean Startup" by Eric Ries: Exploring the principles of lean startup methodology, this book offers practical advice on how to build a successful business by continuously innovating and adapting.

3. "The Startup Owner's Manual" by Steve Blank and Bob Dorf: A comprehensive guide to building a successful startup, covering topics such as customer development, product-market fit, and scaling a business.

4. "Traction: How Any Startup Can Achieve Explosive Customer Growth" by Gabriel Weinberg and Justin Mares: This book provides insights into different marketing strategies and tactics to help businesses gain traction and acquire customers.

5. "The E-Myth Revisited" by Michael E. Gerber: Focusing on the importance of systematizing and scaling a business, this book offers valuable insights for entrepreneurs looking to build a sustainable and successful enterprise.

Tools:

1. LivePlan: An online business planning software that guides users through the process of creating a professional business plan with financial projections, market analysis, and more.

2. Canva: A graphic design platform that offers templates for creating visually appealing business plan documents, including infographics, charts, and presentations.

3. SCORE Business Plan Templates: SCORE, a nonprofit organization dedicated to helping small businesses, provides free business plan templates and resources to assist entrepreneurs in developing their strategic plans.

4. Google Analytics: A powerful tool for tracking website traffic and user behavior, providing valuable insights for developing and optimizing your online marketing strategies.

5. Trello: A project management tool that can be used to organize and track tasks related to business planning, team collaboration, and project execution.

Websites:

1. Small Business Administration (SBA): The SBA website offers a wealth of resources and tools for small business owners, including business planning guides, financial assistance programs, and local resources.

2. Bplans.com: A website offering free sample business plans, articles, and resources to help entrepreneurs create and refine their business strategies.

3. Entrepreneur.com: A popular online resource for business news, articles, and advice on various aspects of entrepreneurship, including business planning, marketing, and management.

4. Investopedia: An educational website providing insights into financial markets, investing, and business strategies, offering articles and tutorials on topics related to business planning and financial management.

5. HubSpot Academy: A platform offering free online courses on inbound marketing, sales, and business growth, providing valuable insights for developing effective marketing and sales strategies for your business.

By utilizing these diverse resources, you can enhance your business planning process, gain valuable insights, and increase your chances of creating a successful and sustainable business venture. Remember, thorough research, strategic thinking, and continuous learning are key components of developing a winning business plan.

Further Reading and Study Recommendations

Once you have completed the comprehensive guide on how to write a business plan, there are numerous resources available to further enhance your knowledge and skills in this crucial aspect of business development. Here are some recommendations for further reading and study:

1. "Business Model Generation" by Alexander Osterwalder and Yves Pigneur: This book provides a practical framework for developing and innovating business models. It offers valuable insights into identifying opportunities, creating value propositions, and designing sustainable business models.

2. "The Lean Startup" by Eric Ries: This book introduces the concept of lean startup methodology, emphasizing the importance of rapid prototyping, customer feedback, and iterative development. It is a must-read for entrepreneurs looking to build successful and scalable businesses.

3. "Value Proposition Design" by Alexander Osterwalder, Yves Pigneur, Gregory Bernarda, and Alan Smith: This book delves into the process of creating compelling value propositions that resonate with customers. It offers tools and techniques for designing value propositions that drive customer engagement and loyalty.

4. "Venture Deals" by Brad Feld and Jason Mendelson: For those interested in understanding the intricacies of venture capital and startup financing, this book provides a comprehensive guide to navigating the world of venture deals, term sheets, and investor negotiations.

5. "The Art of the Start 2.0" by Guy Kawasaki: This book offers practical advice and insights for launching a successful startup, covering topics such as pitching your business, building a strong team, and leveraging social media for marketing and growth.

6. "Running Lean" by Ash Maurya: This book provides a step-by-step guide to applying lean startup principles to validate business ideas, iterate on product development, and build a scalable business model. It is a valuable resource for entrepreneurs seeking to minimize risk and maximize success.

7. "HBR Guide to Building Your Business Case" by Raymond Sheen and Amy Gallo: This Harvard Business Review guide offers practical tips and tools for developing a compelling business case to support decision-making and secure buy-in from stakeholders. It is essential for crafting persuasive arguments and strategies in a business context.

8. "Start with Why" by Simon Sinek: This book explores the concept of starting with a clear sense of purpose and vision in business. It emphasizes the importance of defining your 'why' to inspire customers, employees, and partners and drive long-term success.

In addition to books, there are various online resources, courses, and workshops available to further deepen your understanding of business planning, strategy development, and entrepreneurship. Websites such as Coursera, Udemy, and LinkedIn Learning offer a wide range of courses on business planning, financial modeling, market research, and other relevant topics.

Remember that continuous learning and self-improvement are essential for staying competitive in the dynamic world of business. By exploring these recommended resources and expanding your knowledge base, you can enhance your business planning skills and increase your chances of success in the competitive marketplace.

Printed in Great Britain
by Amazon

47389970R00076